'An inspiring guide to one thing we all want in our lives, a stronger sense of aliveness, purpose and fulfilment.'

Alex Rossi, TV Correspondent

'Andro has the unique experience of working with thousands of the most highly paid, valued and productive people in the world. Her insights are entirely unique given this perspective. If you've ever dreamed about what you would learn if only you could pick the brains of hyper-resourceful leaders, this book is a very close second.'

Daniel Priestly, Entrepreneur, Speaker and Bestselling Author of *Entrepreneur Revolution*

'How would you feel if today was the last day of your life? If you'd like to be capable of answering "fulfilled, happy and contented", read this book.'

Andy Maslen, Author

'*Motivate Yourself* is just like Andro Donovan's consulting (only much less expensive!): very direct, tough, relevant and immediately useful. It gives us tools to discard the damaging and unhelpful thoughts we have within us and to magnify the empowering and liberating ones. Real wisdom here, reading this book is a fantastic investment of time and energy.'

Chairman, Director and Founder Andrew Grene Foundation; Philanthropist

'If you find yourself reflecting on the life you are leading, if you are wanting to create a life with purpose and more meaning, if you simply want to sense check your feelings to better plan your drive to reach self-fulfilment, this is the book for you.'

Lara Morgan, Investor and Entrepreneur

'For all those leaders who've spent years motivating and inspiring others, this book provides a refreshing reminder that happiness and fulfilment come when you invest in your greatest asset: you. An easy read with lots of practical advice on how to be a better you.'

he Reputation Playbook;
;ing Director, Six Degrees

'*Motivate Yourself* is the handbook for action and change, it makes you get up and do it … a must for business men and women, with a warning that it delivers a powerful impact on your life!'

Sally Rustom, Founder and COO of Customer Consulting Ltd

Motivate Yourself

Get the life you want, find purpose and achieve fulfilment

ANDRO DONOVAN

CAPSTONE
A Wiley Brand

This edition first published 2016
© 2016 Andro Donovan

Registered office
John Wiley & Sons Ltd, The Atrium, Southern Gate, Chichester, West Sussex, PO19 8SQ,
United Kingdom

For details of our global editorial offices, for customer services and for information about how
to apply for permission to reuse the copyright material in this book please see our website at
www.wiley.com.

Library of Congress Cataloging-in-Publication Data is available.

A catalogue record for this book is available from the British Library.

ISBN 978-0-857-08690-7 (pbk)
ISBN 978-0-857-08698-3 (ebk) ISBN 978-0-857-08699-0 (ebk)

Cover Design: Wiley
Cover Image: © Melodist/Shutterstock

Set in 11/14 SabonLTStd by Aptara Inc., New Delhi, India
Printed in Great Britain by TJ International Ltd, Padstow, Cornwall, UK

A dedication to my children.
May this book help you to connect to
your own wisdom and love.

Contents

Introduction

....

'I have looked in the mirror every morning and asked myself: "If today were the last day of my life, would I want to do what I am about to do today?" And whenever the answer has been "No" for too many days in a row, I know I need to change something.'

Steve Jobs

THIS IS IT

Wherever you are in your life right now, you may have arrived at the point where you are asking yourself: Is this it?

When you read that statement 'This is it' where are you putting the emphasis?

- This is it? – could mean you are questioning the quality of your life.
- This **is** it – could mean you realize there is no time like the present and life is for living right now.
- **This** is it – could mean you are celebrating a new-found experience.

Where you put the emphasis will reflect how you feel about your life right now!

So many people I meet have a diminished perspective of who they are and what they are capable of. They often completely underestimate what is possible for them in their lives.

In this book, I will be introducing you to tools that have helped hundreds of people break through their limitations and release their true potential.

I have had the privilege of working with thousands of people in over 20 countries; and after 25 years of experience, I can safely say that people fall into roughly speaking five categories. See if you can find yourself in one of the following:

1. You know what you want but are waiting for some future circumstances to happen before you can feel happy and fulfilled.
2. You know what you would like but do not feel you have the ability, confidence or resources to achieve it.
3. You don't know what you want but do know what you don't want.
4. You have lost sight of what's possible and have disengaged and resigned yourself to mediocrity.
5. You know what you want and are going for it but are often hampered by negative thoughts that inhibit your progress or journey.

Whichever category you find yourself in, this book will help you to move forward in a more positive and dynamic way.

So, ask yourself again: 'Why did I pick up this book?' There are a number of reasons and personal circumstances that may have prompted you to seek more motivation, meaning, purpose and fulfilment, so let's spend a little bit of time examining the plethora of reasons that may have prompted you to pick up this book.

- You may have reached a plateau in your life, and you are on a quest for more motivation and drive.
- You may be questioning the meaning of your life and your sense of fulfilment and purpose.
- Perhaps you have started a new job, or you are looking for your first job; maybe you have been made redundant and are having to take a long close look at what you want to do next.

- Perhaps your children have finally flown the nest and you are left with bags more time than you originally had as the lion's share of your life has been focused on looking after your family; now you finally have some time for yourself.
- Perhaps a major event may has caused you to take a harder, more analytical, view of your life.
- You may be simply looking for a boost of energy and drive so that you can start the next phase of your life in a more purposeful way.

Whatever circumstances you find yourself in, this book has the tools to help you motivate yourself, find meaning and discover your purpose, get a greater sense of fulfilment which will accelerate through to the next exciting stage of your life's adventure.

Together, we are going to go on a journey, and we will be travelling through different emotional landscapes until you arrive at a point where you feel ready to get motivated, engaged and purposeful in your life.

All you need to travel is this book and your journal.

How to read this book

I have organized the book into three distinct sections:

1. Discover yourself – A journey to yourself
   Here we explore what lights you up, what makes your life worth living, what you hold most precious and dear.
2. Free yourself – What gets in the way of your happiness?
   Here we will be surfacing all your negative thoughts and feelings that stop you from being the wonderful, self-resourcing person you could be.

Also in this section, we begin the work of re-wiring your existing mindset to make you a motivated and more fulfilled individual.

3. **Motivate your life – Design the life you want to live**

The third and final section provides a step-by-step guide including tools and tips you can implement immediately.

EVERYTHING STARTS WITH A DECISION

Transforming your life is not time related. It starts with a decision and a strong yearning and desire to have it be different, and then follows through with some radical actions.

Many people lack confidence, motivation, or are lost with no clear direction meaning or purpose. They are oblivious to what they are truly capable of. They are often underestimating what is possible for them in their lives.

It may be that they have no job, or it may be that they are a top level CEO; it does not matter where they are or who they are if they are not happy and fulfilled – if they don't experience a strong sense of purpose on some level, their life does not work.

Where they live in the privacy of their own head is what needs to be surfaced and examined.

Once again, ask yourself: Why did you pick up this book? Perhaps part of you is not really satisfied, but you don't dare admit it – not even to yourself – for fear of invalidating your life to date.

Sure you have made some great decisions – after all, you may on the surface have a successful life. You have the luxury to provide the best things that money can buy for your children and family, but still there is something missing.

Part of getting to the answer of some of these deep questions is examining your purpose. It is vital to reconnect to the energy force and your values.

Everyone has values but are not necessarily conscious of them.

Becoming conscious of your values is an essential part of redirecting your focus, and we will be discussing this in much more depth in the first section of the book.

It is my experience that once individuals get a glimpse of what their life could be like, it's like a drug.

Then begins the quest of creating a life where they experience themselves as more fully engaged and expressed.

We race through our lives never pausing to consider who we really are and, more importantly, who we really want to be expressing.

Before I became a facilitator, my career began as an English Literature teacher when I taught in some of the roughest and toughest areas of London.

Here I would meet many teenagers, some of them coming from difficult homes, and I learned very quickly that the first lesson they had to learn was to believe in themselves. I believed that as their teacher I had a responsibility to get them to where they felt confident and strong.

Unfortunately, they had had years of being told:

- you are no good
- you are worthless
- you are bad
- you will never amount to anything.

The difficult ones would end up in 'sin bins' (classrooms manned by strict teachers where the pupil was not allowed to talk or leave the room for the whole day).

Others would be in exclusion units. I realized early on that while the school and teachers felt they were helping, all they were actually doing was supporting the body of evidence these children were gathering about themselves –'I am not good enough, and I am not worthy'.

Getting these pupils to believe in themselves really paid off because, under the hard shell, they were just young people who had been let down and were disillusioned.

Does any of this sound familiar? My work as a facilitator focuses on getting people to stand back and challenge some of their limiting beliefs about what is possible for them. They may have inherited these beliefs from their home life, school life, classroom or cultural background.

However they have acquired these beliefs, they become accustomed to thinking of themselves as smaller than their problems, as victims of circumstance, and generally end up blaming others for their situation or for not having what they want in life. In this paradigm, we are all powerless to effect any change.

'I can't change the direction of the wind, but I can adjust my sails to always reach my destination.'

Jimmy Dean

The big challenge is to get back in touch with what we value, what lights us up, what motivates us in life.

Once this is achieved, we can begin to take a fresh look at every area of our life. We can stand in a place of possibility and choice rather than resignation.

It is my experience that once individuals get a glimpse of who they could be, they become passionate about creating a life where they experience themselves as more fully engaged and expressed.

THE INNOCENCE OF CHILDREN

As children we start out as positive, wide-eyed beings, willing to explore and get things wrong. At this early stage we do not have labels for these experiences, we are not preoccupied with success and failure, we just have experiences from which we learn.

Young children can drop an object from a table over and over again and find the whole process fascinating. Sooner or later the adults in our lives intervene and give us their view of the world. Eventually, we begin to adapt to other people's view of the world and how they view us.

We become preoccupied with seeking approval, conforming or rebelling. Expressing ourselves authentically and dropping the armour-plated coating we have developed to shield us from external criticism, becomes one of our biggest challenges.

Living in the gap
- Are you living 'in the gap' between where you are now and where you want to be?
- Do you yearn to do great things, but ultimately remain in your comfort zone arguing for your limitations?
- Does the experience of fulfilment remain just out of reach, unrequited, like the mythological lovers portrayed in frescos – always chasing the object of their affections but never quite catching them?
- Do you keep yourself stuck by holding on to pain?
- Do you keep part of you hidden from view for fear of being judged, misunderstood or rejected?

 Over to you

Look through these ten questions

Here is a taster of what we will be looking to do – some practical exercises to make this real. Just answer 'Yes' or 'No' to the following statements to find out how much you are living in the gap.

1. There is a part of you that remains hidden and unexpressed for fear of judgement.
2. You are constantly imagining a time in the future when you will be happy, e.g. when you have more money, have a better relationship, more freedom, are slimmer, have a bigger house …
3. You have internal voices that let you know you are not good enough and not worthy.

---

4. You often find yourself withdrawing by sleeping, drinking, smoking, eating, feeling ill, no energy.
5. You wake up feeling exhausted and wishing it was the end of the day when you can sleep.
6. You hate your commute to work.
7. You feel unappreciated by your boss, your husband, your wife …
8. You never have any time for yourself.
9. You can't remember the last time you really had a deep belly laugh and some great fun.
10. You feel unfulfilled and demotivated.

How many times did you answer Yes? The more Yeses you have, the bigger the gap to close!

I come across people all the time who are channelling too much energy into stuff that is not ultimately giving them a sense of satisfaction and fulfilment. They have become caught up in the rat race or are shackled with golden handcuffs in a job that pays well but to which they have sold out for a pension; most importantly **they do not experience choice**, what they do experience is 'having to'.

The best things in life are free but are only available to anyone who has the intention, desire and vision to see beyond their limitations and present circumstances.

'Your present circumstances don't determine where you can go; they merely determine where you start.'

Nido Qubein

THE OUTCOME YOU CAN EXPECT

Do you want your life to be a manifestation of your deepest values, a life where you get to choose consciously where and who you spend your time with?

A life of choice, a life where you are in the driver's seat and you are the author of your universe?

Going through the step-by-step process outlined in this book, you will begin to create clarity and vision for your own life.

'An unexamined life is not worth living.'

Throughout this book, you will be getting opportunities to do precisely this. To re-examine some of your decisions and choices with a view to dismantling old, outdated beliefs, negative self-talk and entrenched mindsets that have rendered you powerless.

In 2013, a fascinating study was performed by Bronnie Ware – a nurse in a terminal palliative care unit.

She decided to poll her patients in their last days in the hope of uncovering any regrets so others might learn. These were her findings:

> 'The regrets touch upon being more genuine, not working so hard, expressing one's true feelings, staying in touch with friends and finding more joy in life.'
>
> Bronnie Ware, author of *The Top 5 Regrets of the Dying* (Hay House)[1]

[1] For more information about Bronnie Ware and *The Top 5 Regrets of the Dying*, visit hayhouse.com.au or bronnieware.com.

My experience aligns with this beautifully, I have sprinkled the book with case studies of people I have worked with who have had similar regrets. Luckily they are not on their deathbed, but they have had a wake up call in their life and are now fully focused on redressing the balance. These regrets are summarized as follows – can you identify with any of them?

1. **Not having the courage to live a life true to yourself and instead living the life others expect of you.**
   Are you living your dreams and honouring your dearest values?

   Are you following your heart or are you living a life to fulfil someone else's dream or to keep their approval? You have the freedom today to choose a different way to live your life. Use this book and the methods to help you journal your way to a better life.

2. **Neglecting those closest to you or taking them for granted.**
   Do you have a spouse and family you are neglecting for the sake of your work? When was the last time you put your kids to bed and read them a bedtime story? Our children are only children for a very short time, are you making memories you can all share today or are you waiting for a time when you are not so busy? 'Time waits for no man' and neither do your children, don't throw away their youth.

3. **Not having the courage to express your feelings.** Are you suppressing your feelings in order to keep peace with others? Are you hiding your true light behind a bushel, never expressing yourself truthfully for fear of offending or causing upset? Are you taking every opportunity to be up to date with your loved ones and friends or are you harbouring bitterness and resentments? Be careful, for what we hold on to holds us back.

4. **Failure to stay in touch with supporting friends and peers.** Friendships are special and take time and investment to nurture and develop. Good friends should never be taken for

granted, staying in touch and keeping the channels open will serve you particularly in the tricky times when you need a listening ear or a shoulder to cry on. Friends celebrate your successes and commiserate with you when times get tough. Never underestimate the value they bring to your life. No man is an island.

5. **Not allowing myself to be happier.**

Happiness is a state of mind and a choice; if we consistently choose to see the glass half empty and moan about what is not great in our life, we blind ourselves to what miracles are happening around us every day. The kindnesses people show us, the beautiful scenery, sunsets, seascapes, forests we can see. When we stop being grateful for our health, family and loved ones we deny others and ourselves the opportunity to express joy and happiness. This is not something we should only leave for Christmas; we should do every day of our lives. Beware of getting stuck in a habitual way of expressing yourself. Don't be scared to show your emotions, stop pretending that you are OK with things as they are and if you are not happy, change it.

 Over to you

Which regret do you struggle with most?

What is holding you back?

Don't wait for a life-threatening disease or a deathbed moment to get your insight, start NOW.

As I said, it's your decision, but using the tools in this book to give you the insights, and then applying what you learn, will help you to make that change. My desired outcome for you is that at the end of this journey I will guide you through you will arrive at a new stage and will be stating one of the following:

- My priorities have completely changed.
- I now feel I can really follow my hopes and dreams.
- I want to focus on happiness.
- I want to express my true self.
- I am ready to follow my dreams.
- I have a new sense of meaning and purpose.

This book is a distillation of years of experience, seminars I have run and attended, books I have read and amazing people I have learned from on my path.

I want you to enjoy this book, and also be able to use it to motivate yourself, connect to your purpose, and get what you really want out of life.

Grab your journal. Let's get started.

Andro Donovan.

PART ONE

Discover Yourself:
A Journey to You

1

Mind Your Values

··

'Those who look outside dream, those who look inside awake.'

Carl Jung

At the heart of a truly fulfilling personal and business life there will always be a set of strong core values. The question is: Do you ever give yourself the time and permission to stop and ask yourself what matters to you?

DISCOVERING YOUR ESSENTIAL VALUES

Becoming more conscious of your values gives a strong sense of identity for you, your life and your career. If you have chosen a career that is a vehicle for generating money, but does not provide you with any personal satisfaction, maybe it's time to reconsider. Values provide focus and direction for (in this instance) financial success and give your desires more meaning.

So what about you? Let me ask you again: How do you feel about getting connected to your true values so that you can live a life that will make you happy and fulfilled?

I warn you, this process can be life changing. You may change your business, re-evaluate your friendships and find your soulmate, take better care of your health and show more affection to those around you. Ultimately, it will be your choice. With values comes choice. With choice comes change. And with change comes growth.

Now, how do you feel about leaping into the world of values? Ready? Put your mind, body and soul into first gear and let's go!

WHAT ARE VALUES?

What drives most people is a yearning to improve the quality of their lives while at the same time remaining true to themselves. Becoming conscious of what fundamentally drives you is not always obvious. While you are busy running on the treadmill of life, you will undoubtedly miss and potentially suppress those hidden drivers that are a powerful force within you.

Connecting to your deepest values, the ones you hold most dear, will give you the renewed energy, motivation and impetus to live your life more fully.

Consider the following questions:
- What is my life's purpose?
- What is my unique contribution?
- What will I be remembered for?
- What makes me feel alive and vital on this planet?

These four questions will be answered over the course of the book, starting from the position of values.

While answering these questions you will inadvertently start to connect to what is important to you, the quality or essence you can't live without. Although you may have been hitherto unaware of these hidden drivers, not knowing them can be – in the worst case scenario – a contributing factor to an overall sense of meaninglessness.

Many people tend to chase goals only to find that when they achieve them there is a strong sense of anticlimax. When this happens, they get a fleeting moment of happiness and joy that is rapidly followed by 'what's the next question?' Living a life that is disconnected from your values may lead you to pursue goals that will not ultimately satisfy nor nourish you longer term.

It's a bit like going for a sugary treat or pick-me-up when we are hungry for a proper meal. We go for the biscuit or bag of crisps only to find out we are still hungry. We have not been properly nourished so we begin to crave more and more junk food that will never feel satisfying.

Connecting to your core values and activating them in your day-to-day life is the fastest way to feel nourished and the most motivating and direct route to personal fulfilment and satisfaction.

Values act like a compass and guide you towards your life's purpose and true north. Values are your pure essence – that which is you and your essential self. Knowing your values and acting in accordance with them provides focus and direction in the choices you make, the roles you take on, the jobs you choose and the way you use your leisure time.

EXPRESSING YOUR ESSENTIAL VALUES

One of the most life-enhancing exercises I have ever done was getting in touch with my key drivers and values and then *creating a life where I experienced and expressed them on a daily basis*. This does not happen overnight; it is an ongoing process, where the learning comes from the journey rather than reaching the ultimate destination.

When I first started to contemplate the bigger 'why' questions, I thought I knew who I was and what my values were, but I didn't. My mentor kick-started a process that set me on a highway to confusion armed with only a set of abstract adjectives: you name it, I valued it. I valued courage, honesty, respect and integrity. However, none of these were, in reality, my core values and they were in fact utterly meaningless. They were too easy to choose.

In the ensuing personal chaos, I felt deflated and as though I was on a roundabout with no clearly marked exit signs. When I tried to work out which direction I should travel in, all the roads seemed equally inviting yet somehow closed. At every junction there was a roadblock or another dead end. As I turned to face another potential road, misleading signposts appeared everywhere. Then, and only then, did I put on the brakes and allow myself to connect to the essence of who I thought I was.

I have come to realize that life is an adventure, and this has helped me to grow as a person, as a mother, as a facilitator and as an executive coach. Today I am clear about what my values are. I know what the most effective means are to fast-track me to achieving them and what the end result of remaining faithful to the essential me is.

Imagine living every day with a certain inner knowledge and allowing your values to pull you effortlessly along an invisible thread towards a life of fulfilment.

My watershed moment – A fish can love a bird but where will they live?

Have you ever felt like a fish out of water? As a young woman fresh out of college deciding on what to do for my gap year, I remember believing that 'girls like me do not go backpacking around the world'. I came from a very sheltered and conservative background. Girls like me did not go travelling to strange countries unescorted. It would be far too dangerous and inappropriate for a single girl. No, what we do is find a nice steady job, just to get some useful work experience, preferably not too far from home.

This is precisely what I did. I obtained a job in a local government careers office. My job entailed interviewing young people and cajoling them to go for a job or, if I could not place them in any of the available jobs, signing them up for benefits. This role provided me with two amazing insights:

First: I realized that the part of the job I enjoyed most was spotting the hidden talent and potential of these youngsters. Helping them to create a better life than the one they seemed destined to lead. Rescuing them from a life of benefits to a life of employment and contribution gave me a strong sense of purpose.

Second: I did not fit into the environment I found myself in. Everyone around me was a civil servant working out how they could have a sick day or a training day to get out of working. It was not so much that they were demotivated; they were just playing the system for anything they could get away with. It was an entrenched culture that was at loggerheads with everything I believed in. They were not dishonest or bad people; they just did not seem to want much out of life. It appeared to me that they were happy in their 9 to 5 mentality.

It was a huge challenge in this stale culture to get any buy-in for creative new ideas. The attitude that I was constantly faced with was 'that's not the way we do things around here'! I realized that although I had learned a lot about myself, I needed to get out before I got sucked into the same mindset. I was a fish out of water who couldn't get enough oxygen into my system. I needed to utilize my emerging talents in a different environment. I longed to explore new oceans and gain new perspectives, but it was as if I had to swim quietly and safely to get through the day. I very rapidly outgrew this particular fish bowl.

I wanted to make a bigger contribution. So I enrolled at university to read English and Education. My driver? If I could qualify as a teacher, I could help educate young people to demand a better future. At 18, I had a strong need to make a CONTRIBUTION. Contribution became my compass.

Identifying my compass occurred almost by accident, which is often the way things happen. But it became one of my essential values and remains to this day a primary driving force in my life. Through this experience I discovered my 'why', and 'why' values are such important guiding principles for life choices and decisions.

 Your million dollar questions

Read the following questions several times and then take yourself for a walk and a breath of fresh air. When you come back, consider your answers:

- How do I know what my values are?

Consider for a moment what lights you up. Get out a pen and paper and ask:

- What gets you out of bed in the morning?
- What do you love doing with your spare time?
- What are your favourite hobbies?
- Where do you like to travel to and why?
- What films or books move you deeply?

As you reflect on your answers you will begin to arrive at what is essentially important to you. Make sure you record your answers in your journal as you go through the practical exercises in this book. Remember that your core values are your internal, essential compass for satisfaction, fulfilment, meaning and purpose. When you act from your core values, you are operating at your highest level. Everyone has a higher level and a lower level of being (highest self and lower self) as you will discover in the following chapter. However, you may not be aware of this all the time. Gathering to mind a number of these experiences will help you to begin to get in touch with your spiritual drive that is harnessed through your values and comes from your highest self.

When you are at your best, feeling invincible, happy and purposeful, this is when you are living your values.

SAME QUESTION, DIFFERENT ANGLES

You have to ask yourself the same question over and over again from different angles for it to make sense – e.g. what do I love doing? When am I at my most happy? Who do I like to be around? Why? –because values are multi-dimensional.

One of the aspects of my career that nourishes me on a daily basis is the letters and testimonials I receive from satisfied clients. Clients who tell me that as a result of a seminar they have had a life-changing experience or a realization that has made them change direction or has transformed a self-limiting mindset. When I receive this feedback, my need to make a difference and a contribution is fully activated.

Ask yourself: What activates any of your values so that they nourish and quench the hunger in you?

What activates your values?

Everyone connects to experiences in different ways. For some it might be a visual experience, for others sound, for others feeling, and maybe some will relate to other senses. Let's make a start with something as ordinary as watching a film. Have you ever thought about why some films move you and others leave you cold? It is because they connect emotionally to the essence of you, to something you hold dear. It could be the amazing visuals, incredible soundtrack or brilliant story and acting that reminds you of times past or dreams long forgotten. It might evoke memories of a meal and all the associated flavours, or a holiday romance.

It's the same with a book. A film or a book (or even a talk) can really inspire you to take action. You will have come across many worthy causes, but there will be something about *this* particular one that triggers you at a deeper level. When triggered, you are moved because you resonate with the energy of the message. It's a compelling motivator. Why? Because it speaks to a deep value, connects you emotionally, and you identify with aspects of the theme. For example, in the film *The Remains of the Day* when the central character, the loyal butler played by Anthony Hopkins, places duty above love, he subsequently ends his days isolated and lonely. If this theme moves you it could be because you identify with the central figure and his predicament. Films/books that deeply move us may give us an indication of our deeper values.

 Over to you

Films/books that move you

1. Start by thinking about your top five films. If films aren't your thing, choose books. Not necessarily the most recent ones, but the ones that you could watch (or read) over and over again, because they inspire you in some way.
2. Now consider what it was about these films that moved and inspired you, lifted your spirits and sparked a yearning.
3. Now write down some of the values those films encapsulate.

If a film or book doesn't immediately come to mind, look back through your DVD collection (or bookshelf) and make a date to enjoy a film tonight.

Some examples to help you:

The Shawshank Redemption is a film about the strength of the human spirit, dignity, having a vision and purpose that transcends the prison walls, friendship and loyalty.

Schindler's List is about the courage, selflessness and integrity of one human being who saved Jews from the gas chamber in spite of the risk to himself.

Your turn

1. The film (or book) ... Value/values it represents for me
2. The film (or book) ... Value/values it represents for me
3. The film (or book) ... Value/values it represents for me
4. The film (or book) ... Value/values it represents for me
5. The film (or book) ... Value/values it represents for me

Can you see how, by consciously distilling your essential values, you can build a meaningful and purposeful direction in your life? Of course, some of these values will be inherited from parents, school, culture and faith. However, you are not your parents, so it's worth actively taking ownership of those values that serve you now. This single action will catapult you along a new and more meaningful path. Imagine how exciting it will be to choose to back the values that represent who you are today and the way you want to be defined. How does it feel? What other visuals or sounds do you get when you think about this?

When you are truly operating from your highest values, you feel a strong sense of being on the right path. You don't feel lost or foggy but clear and purposeful. Your values become your compass for life. Without awareness of your compass, you can easily lose your way.

IS THIS YOU?

I have worked with some people who reach a certain point in their lives and suddenly realize that they have invested a lot of energy chasing the wrong things. They may have tons of 'form', i.e. material things like houses, cars, or holiday homes, but they do not experience satisfaction or fulfilment. They are the proverbial rat on the treadmill of life set to an ever-increasing speed. They have become victims of their need for constant achievement. Their overheads are so high they have to keep making money to fuel the machine.

'I was living the life my parents had designed for me' – Deepak

One of my clients arrived at one of my retreats feeling exhausted by the life he had created. While doing the values work, he acknowledged that his top value was FAMILY. However, he was concerned about the relationship he had with his wife: it had become flat and had lost its spark. He only saw his wife during school holidays and vacations as his business, which needed him, was in Africa. He wanted the best education money could buy so he decided to put his older kids in English private boarding schools. His wife, in the meantime, lived in London with his younger daughter. She wanted to be close to the children should they need her. He realized that, while his businesses were thriving, he had set up his life to neglect his biggest priority, his family.

Deepak came from a wealthy and privileged Indian family. All his life he had been the good son doing what was expected of him in his culture and family. Being the firstborn son, he carried the burden of duty to continue the business that had been in his family for many generations before.

One day he attended one of my retreats, and I watched him struggle with the question 'what do you want out of life'? He told me it was not a question he could answer easily as he did not get to choose. Through the process of life planning, he came to realize he was living the life someone else had designed for him. His whole life had been a 'should' and a 'must'. However, no one had ever taken the time to ask Deepak what his heart's desire was for fear he would take a direction away from the running of the family business.

At that moment, he made a radical decision. *'If I want to be free I need to find a responsible CEO to navigate the ship while I go away and do what I want to do.'* Deepak had always had a desire to be a consultant coach to other businesses. He was finally committed to making some radical changes.

Deepak's life to that date was about fulfilling his parent's expectations, but he never once considered *what* he wanted. Now he is.

When is a yacht not a yacht?

Being more conscious of your values assists you in activating your true powers and gifts. Wanting a great car or house, yacht or the best education is fine as long as you know which value it is helping you manifest.

Imagine if you had a strong desire to own a yacht. It may be that you simply want to show off. Alternatively, on a deeper level, you may want a sense of freedom, adventure and of being at one with the elements while you sail the seas. For everyone, it is recognizing what values your desires trigger that gives meaning to the 'form' items you crave. When you think about a yacht now, I bet it has taken on a completely different meaning. It is essential for you to consider what you want as much as why, as it's there to serve a deeper, stronger purpose; in other words, it's not just bling! As you have already seen, getting down to what your essential value drivers are is a prerequisite to understanding why you want the things you do.

If you become a 'form junkie' you can lose sight of what's important to you and become cut off from the bit that sustains you, e.g. the pursuit of money and status may end up alienating your family. So understanding what's important to you helps you prioritize and create balance in your life.

Once you have reconnected to your essential values you can choose your direction and stop being a victim of the circumstances you find yourself in. You can take an active role. You are in the driver's seat, so to speak, rather than a passenger who has no control of where the car will end up. What you aspire to depends on what you perceive you need to be fulfilled. Life is a bit of a balancing act. When you get one thing right, other things can go out of kilter. However, when you are connected to your essence or inner spirit and true to yourself – that is when your true values surface.

It is important to remember that it is not the number of values that is key, but the strength of their meaning. That is why discovering your dominant values is a practical way to know that you are going in the right direction and are on track to fulfilling your purpose. It is those values that, like your DNA, make you unique!

The Dalai Lama, when asked what surprised him most about humanity, answered:

> 'Man, he sacrifices his health in order to make money. Then he sacrifices money to recuperate his health. Then he is so anxious about the future that he does not enjoy the present: the result being that he does not live in the present or the future; he lives as though he is never going to die, and then he dies having never really lived.'

Arriving at the answer to what your core values are is a fundamental step towards a better, happier, more congruent life. Some people have to wait for a life-threatening illness that gives them a complete change of perspective. Is that you?

THE JOURNEY TO THE INNER SELF

You have already considered your top five films (books) and have made a start into the world of your essential values. You should have a longish list of values that you identified from the films.

Values trangression

Sometimes you become most aware of your values when you see them being transgressed. This is normal, and it is one of the things that I would ask you to look out for. Some of these might have come up as you were watching a film. Alternatively, maybe there is something currently happening that moves you. What is causing you pain or irritation? What are the causes that stir you? Think about the people that wound you. Add these values to your film values list.

 Over to you

Identifying your top five to eight values

Step 1
- Think of someone you admire, a celebrity, historical figure or a member of your family or a member of your peer group.
- Think of a quality (or qualities) this person has.
- What is it about them that inspires you?

What you have written down are some of your highest values, and they are a mirror of you at your best. You would not be attracted to these qualities unless you valued them. You may struggle to express these qualities fully but, ultimately, when you are activating these you are plugged into that energy. Meet yourself, as this is you at your best and highest self.

A Return To Love (1992) by Marianne Williamson is a beautiful poem that was used at Nelson Mandela's 1994 inaugural address. Every time I read it I am moved, because it speaks to me at a deep level. Go to this URL (https:// Marianne.com/ a-return-to-love) and read it, reflect and journal what comes up for you.

The main principle here is that what scares us is our huge potential rather than our limitations. And it is the qualities we most admire in others that are a direct mirror of our own highest qualities. So, for instance, if you admire someone for their great courage, what you are connecting to is your courage which you may have not fully expressed as yet.

Step 2

You might find a walk or some reflection time helps before you start.

Looking down at your film (book) list and at the causes and the qualities you wrote for the people you admire list:

- Distill this list into your top values, ensuring they are important to you (you may need to do this several times).
- Now choose five to eight values you wish to focus on, e.g. love, contribution, etc.

Step 3
CLARIFYING QUESTIONS

Once you have listed your values, put them through the filter of these questions. This will help make your values three dimensional. If you can't come up with answers easily, maybe you need to rethink which values would be in your top five to eight.

- Why is this value important in my life?
- Who benefits when I am expressing this value?
- How do I feel about myself when I am activating this value?
- How do I feel when I am disconnected from this value?

Step 4

Record your core value statements. Here is an example.

Love

This value is important in my life, it manifests when I am connected to my centre. When I express love, I feel whole, authentic and at one with the universe and everyone in it. It diminishes when I am cut off, hurt, angry and feeling judged.

When I express love, I am strong, powerful, invincible. When I disconnect from it everything around me is dull, diminished and I feel isolated, so much so it's difficult to breathe.

Love is my vital life source; therefore, I must stay connected to it and look for opportunities to express it. When I express love I am coming from my highest self; I am operating out of my Angel – I have wings. I am defenceless, vulnerable, open. I am pure light and energy.

Distill one or two of your top values into a statement like the one above about how you will express this value in your life. Use the clarifying questions in Step 3 to help you articulate your value statement.

Step 5
Once you have your values, define what they mean to you AND how they will manifest in your life.

- How will you activate these values in your day-to-day life?
- How will others see you living your values?

Once you have identified your core values, the next step is to activate them as a priority in your life. Having values is one thing, but expressing and living them is quite another. This way you will be being true to yourself, rather than living the life others expect of you. Living your values becomes your organizing principle, it will simplify and focus you on what is most important and fulfilling.

In the next chapter, we will be further exploring how being conscious of your values directly guides you towards articulating your purpose.

Key thinking points

- What were your five to eight values and why?
- What would it mean if you were to incorporate at least one of them starting right now?
- How do your values differ to the ones you thought you had at the beginning of the chapter?
- What would it mean if you couldn't live your life according to your values?
- What is the one action you will take as a result of reading this chapter?

Practise this mantra

'I allow my values to guide me every day.'

2

Expressing Your Highest Self: Finding Your Purpose

'Twenty years from now you will be more disappointed by the things that you didn't do than by the ones you did do, so throw off the bowlines, sail away from safe harbor, catch the trade winds in your sails. Explore, Dream, Discover.'

Mark Twain

Expressing Your Highest Self: Finding Your Purpose

Without a doubt, once you get connected to your core values, your compass will slowly guide you towards your purpose. Imagine that, no matter who you are or where you find yourself, you discover, because of your values, the stirrings of a yearning for purpose. On that journey towards fulfilment, the fundamental contemplation always comes back to:

WHAT IS MY PURPOSE?

Having a defined purpose delivers a context that encourages and motivates you to persevere even when the going gets tough. Purpose gives meaning to your life and helps to strengthen your resolve.

The quest to find meaning and purpose is at the root of all cultures, religions and civilizations since time immemorial. Our fairy tales are rooted in the central character having a mission or purpose – the prince in *Cinderella* has to find the girl who can fit into the golden slipper so he can marry her and live happily ever after.

When we were children, the first thing we asked a gang of kids when we wanted to join in was always 'what game are you playing?' Children need to know the purpose of a game at its simplest level, e.g. do we need to run to the woods and back without being caught? This simple parameter, once understood, can keep a gang of kids playing for hours.

At the heart of every major step change in our history was a stated purpose that contextualized an otherwise outlandish activity. Think of the suffragettes chaining themselves to the railings of government buildings: they were fighting for women to have the vote. Without this stated purpose, there would be no point or meaning to the hardships the suffragettes were prepared to endure in its name.

THE HEROIC ENERGY OF PURPOSE

We can all name major leaders who had incredible purpose. Martin Luther King, one of the most lauded African-American leaders in history with his civil rights vision, often referenced through his 1963 speech 'I have a dream ...'; Nelson Mandela with his quest for anti-apartheid, encouraging people to 'release themselves from fear and liberate others'; Winston Churchill rallying the country to win the war with his cry 'we'll fight them on the beaches ...'.

Purpose makes mere mortals invincible, fearless and charismatic. One man who had an impact on me in the 80s was Bob Geldof. His finest moment was when he was on a mission to 'Feed the World'. Geldof and co-writer Midge Ure's first version of 'Do They Know It's Christmas?' raised millions for famine relief in Ethiopia. His purpose inspired leaders, celebrities and politicians to follow his lead. At this time in his life he was fearless, strong and inspiring and nobody could get in his way. He captured the imagination and unified a worldwide audience, which cut through culture, religion and beliefs. Everybody wanted to be part of it.

This strong and powerful conscious call to action demonstrates the ability of purpose to motivate. An action taken with some purpose behind it creates meaning.

The well-remembered leaders and heroes of our culture all had a purpose, which emotionally connects followers and inspires them to follow.

We can't all be Bob Geldof, Mandela or Churchill I hear you say!

Perhaps not; but in our own way we either create purpose and turn the seemingly ordinary into a worthwhile task, or we stay ordinary. Having a purpose takes us out of mediocrity into a world of worthy challenges and possibility. Some of the happiest, most fulfilled people I know are those who are in service to others. Conversely, when there is not a clear purpose that drives us, our lives can become empty and meaningless.

Have you heard the story of three people digging a hole?

A man walking down the road notices three men digging holes in the ground. All three men are involved in the same task but are digging with very different energy. The first man seems apathetic and bored and is not putting much energy into it.

The man asks him, 'What are you doing?'

He says, 'What does it look like, I'm digging a hole!'

The second man is digging with more energy. 'What are you doing?'

'I am building a wall.'

The third man is digging with enthusiasm and great focus; he has a smile on his face.

'What are you doing?'

'I am building a cathedral!'

The meaning we attach to our purpose is directly reflected in the energy we invest and our involvement in the task. This drives our motivation to continue.

'I wanted to die, to just give up, and then I saw the faces of my children' – Joe

One of my clients was a successful entrepreneur in the prime of his life; he had four children a beautiful wife and a great life. He also had a penchant for motorbikes. One of his many adventures was a motorbike trip to Africa. If you are a biker, you will know that desire for the freedom and challenges that come with the speed of an open road.

Out on the road, he was enjoying the speed and exhilaration of riding his motorcycle when all of a sudden a van came towards him on the wrong side of the road. The impact of the collision flung him up in the air. The crash left him semi-conscious, crushed, and with dismembered pieces of his body lying in the road. In a painful state of confusion, he didn't know what had happened, and could not contemplate what would happen next. The driver didn't stop and left him, now unconscious, to his fate.

In hospital, during his operation, he felt himself slipping away; he saw the doctors shaking their heads indicating all hope was gone. At that moment, he saw a warm white light beckoning him to leave the painful place that was his human body and allow himself to be drawn into the healing glow.

Then he felt the presence of his children calling him and pulling him back. They were not ready to let him go.

When he came to, he was in hospital listening to the doctor say: 'We really thought we had lost you. It's a miracle you have survived; we were about to give up on you. However I am afraid you have lost a leg and your right arm as well as one of your kidneys.' Finding the courage to go through 20 operations and carry on took a lot of personal determination and resilience.

Instead of being overcome with despair and giving up it was his love of his family, a purpose beyond his own needs, that gave him the courage and spiritual energy to find the strength to carry on. This traumatic experience destroyed his marriage and sadly he divorced. In spite of the fact that he was now disabled and single, he used his devastating experience to make an enormous contribution to others who found themselves in similar circumstances.

He has created a Foundation that gives help and assistance to people who have gone through similar experiences.

He now shares his life with a beautiful young woman, who has become the love of his life and who has just delivered a gorgeous blond-haired, blue-eyed son. Looking back, Joe now values his accident as he sees it as a necessary path that led him to finally finding the love of his life and his purpose: to give back, be of service and help the less fortunate.

Joe's story illustrates that having a bigger purpose, beyond our own selfish needs, can drive us to express enormous courage and endurance against all odds. Having a compelling purpose brings out the best in us. You will surely know of other stories just like this and may well have been through a life-changing experience yourself.

PURPOSE IS CONTAGIOUS

Have you noticed how purpose is contagious? When people have purpose they tend to be very excited about their life. More importantly, we want to be around them because they are energetic, optimistic, driven and cheerful in spite of the hardships they may be enduring. **Do you know anyone like that?**

Conversely, people who have no vision or purpose in their life may spend a disproportionate amount of time moaning, blaming others for their circumstances and quite honestly draining us of our energy. These are the sorts of people we want to avoid. **Do you know people like that?**

Purpose is not only for heroes

Mums and dads can make bringing up their kids an inspiring purpose; they do it brilliantly, take them to the park, play with them and give them attention, take pleasure in cooking their favourite meals. These are very worthy purposes.

Purpose does not need to be a high-level challenge like 'I am going to save the planet!' But if your purpose gets you out of bed in the morning and you experience real meaning and value in what you do then that's great.

It's not what you do; it's the way that you do it and the meaning you attach to it.

People with purpose are more driven, excited and energized about their life, whatever it may be. Having a vision or a dream of where you want to get to in life gives you energy, determination and a direction.

So how do I go about connecting to my purpose?

So what if you have arrived at a point in your life where you are questioning what your life is about? Where you feel the needle on your compass is stuck. Maybe you have lost sight of your meaning and purpose. Sometimes an event can rock our world to the point where we are rendered lost, bereft and have lost all sense of meaning. Losing a loved one, a painful break up, a bankrupt business. There are a number of circumstances that can disconnect us from our true direction and purpose.

Just like trees, we need a deeper root structure if we are to survive the storms and gales of life. Clear, defined values, a mission and a direction give us deeper roots so that we have the courage to pick ourselves up and carry on even when all seems lost – like Joe.

It may be that you have not had a devastating experience; you may be thinking 'I have got everything, a lovely wife/husband beautiful kids a good lifestyle ...', but you know something is missing.

The feeling that things are not quite right may initially start as a faint whisper. At times the inner whisper calling us to connect to our purpose is almost inaudible, and at other times it's a thundering roar from within. The inner voice remains constant even though we may try to ignore it, and it never stops trying to get our attention.

Consider the times when you have ignored this voice: What happened? I am guessing more of the stuff you didn't want, and regrets over the fact that you should have backed your instinct? This voice I shall refer to as your highest self; and it is the part of you that is your best counsel and expresses itself most clearly when you are living your values.

When you are united and at one with this voice, you automatically tune into your highest self. Your highest self is you, your inner consciousness. Imagine another you, without the limiting human conditioning that can get in the way of your otherwise courageous self. Imagine a you devoid of negativity and boundless, with infinite capability. The highest self only wants the best for you; if only you would open your heart and hear what 'higher you' has to say. Now imagine that highest self watching you lead your busy, frenetic life and wondering when you are going to take heed.

This part of you lives above the panic, noise and stress and is your best council in times of need. Connection to this highest self, or inner wisdom if you will, is a spiritual quest. Our highest self is the part of us that embodies the values we hold most dear. Our spiritual drive, as discussed in Chapter 1, comes from a deeply held set of values and is the most powerful, life-changing energy we can link into. Spiritual energy is having the courage to back our values against all odds.

Over to you

Spotting the difference between head and heart

Below I have highlighted some common definitions of the highest self. Please select the one that you feel most comfortable with, or you may have your own definition. Connect to whichever one has meaning for you for the purposes of the following processes and exercises.

> **Your spirit** – your true essence, that voice which guides and encourages you to be your best self and most capable you. That part of you that lives your values and backs your principles even when it may mean losing approval or disempowering friendships.
>
> Depending on your belief system, some people refer to this part of themselves as **God's voice**. This is the voice they tap into in prayer and worship. Worship is a kind of meditation to quiet the noise in your head and tune into a spiritual connection with God.
>
> **Gut instinct** – that feeling that people get when they can't explain why but they know something is right or something is wrong.
>
> **Heart** – when people talk about coming from their heart or listening to their heart they are referring once again to this part of themselves that is wise and always knows best. Its guiding principle is love, and when we come from love for ourselves we normally make better choices.
>
> **Heart and soul** – a common way of referring to what you know is good for you deep down in your inner core.

As you can see, there are many definitions and ways we can tap into our inner voice. However, what about the other voices that we hear when we are feeling fear? These are the times when we are tuning into our survival voices, e.g. 'How do I get out of here', or 'I can't do x or y'. This is your small, disempowering head voice that keeps you stuck and in your comfort zone. I will be discussing these voices more fully in Part Two.

Get comfortable and let's explore how you can spot the difference between highest self voice and head voice.

1. Remember a time when you had to make a choice in life but felt torn between your highest self and your small, head self. Consider why you went with your small self while ignoring the guidance of your highest self. Jot down in your journal what happened and how you felt about yourself.

Think of a time where you felt strongly and powerfully guided to make a decision, or to take a path that led you somewhere great – even though at the time you may have had fear, doubt and uncertainty. Jot down in your journal what happened and how you felt about having listened to your highest self.

Learning to tune into that voice, which comes from your essence, is a good way to strengthen your purpose. We all have the ability to be a wise counsel to ourselves, but so often we are too caught up in our busyness and our own immediate survival mode to hear.

Creating regular rituals where you decompress and tune into your inner wisdom will result in you eventually feeling that you can tap into your highest self voice whenever you need to. Many people who meditate get answers to very big questions in this space.

> **Connecting with your essence – your highest self**
>
> Read these questions and reflect on what comes up for you.
>
> - Do you want to feel more alive and engaged?
> - Do you want to express yourself fully and authentically?
> - Do you want to experience more excitement, motivation and purpose every day?
> - Do you want to contribute to others without self-interest?
> - What is the cost of not living in alignment with your purpose?

We have already established in Chapter 1 that values are who we are at our core; our essence if you will. As we discovered, values are unique and individual; when we activate our values it is our most fulfilling form of expressing and relating. Our values serve as a compass, pointing out what it means to be true to oneself. When we honour our values on a regular and consistent basis, we honour our highest self and life is good and fulfilling. Your highest self speaks to you from a deep place within and is not limited by your belief system. This voice does not come from your small, head self; it comes from the depths of your heart.

 Over to you

Connecting to your spiritual energy

1. Find a quiet space and think of a time when you felt a oneness with the planet, a relationship with a power bigger than yourself. A moment in time when you had an experience of being moved to tears you were so

overwhelmed by joy and connection. These are some examples I have heard on from my clients: seeing my baby being born, a deep experience of being at one with nature, the sea, a miraculous mountain view, an angelic choir singing, a strong sense of unconditional love for a pet.

2. Get comfortable in your chair, close your eyes, and imagine this time in your life. Notice where you are: Who is with you? Notice the quality of light. Notice the sights and sounds and smells.

3. Bring this memory alive and actually be in it now. Feel what you were feeling, see what you saw and hear what you heard. Are you aware of any smells? What else do you notice?

4. Jot down in your journal how you feel about yourself and the world, e.g. love, oneness, joy, peace and connection.

5. Note the key emotions and feelings you had. Remember that the words are just identifiers, the experience of being in touch with and honouring your spiritual connection is the point.

Everyone's idea of spiritual connection is different. However, the most common factor is a deep sense of caring and love. There is a common desire from people of all walks of life, culture and faith to connect with the power of love. The more time you invest in connecting to your spiritual energy, the more happy, satisfied and fulfilled you will be. This connection helps you create the clarity that makes more difficult questions easier to answer, such as am I in the right relationship, job, environment? It moves your compass a point closer to your purpose.

LOVE WHAT YOU DO AT WORK

Some people are lucky enough to have found a career that feeds their soul on a regular basis. I feel very fortunate to have always been in the field of education. As mentioned in the values chapter, one of my top values is **contribution** and making a difference. It is very convenient, therefore, being a coach/facilitator for the simple reason that I get to live this value every day at work. Every time I get one of my clients back on their path, or they have had an insight that results in a decision to change their life in some way where they will have more satisfaction and fulfillment, I have achieved my purpose.

When all is said and done, most of us spend a lot of our life at work. If you are dragging yourself into a job that you resent, a job where you are sacrificing everything that really matters to you, e.g. quality time with your wife/husband and kids, a job where you feel you have to disconnect from your heart and soul to get through the day as it's so dehumanizing, unpleasant and stressful that you have to cut off from that part of you that is you to get through the day, then you really have to question – **is it worth it?**

Finding your path and what you are passionate about is not always clear. I have heard people refer to certain careers as 'a calling'. The jobs that are described in this way are often teaching, medicine or nursing, but as far as I am concerned any job that gives you a sense of satisfaction and gives you an opportunity to express some of your values is a job worth doing.

Whatever job you do, make sure it gives you meaning and allows you to express the real you.

FINDING PURPOSE ELSEWHERE

If you are questioning whether you are in the right job, struggling to find meaning in your existing employment or have reached a point where you are ready for a change, then the following processes can help you find alternatives that dovetail with your purpose and nourish your soul.

Wherever you find yourself in your life right now, for instance if you are unemployed, retired, or a stay at home mum, dad or a carer, the following may also help you discover how you could usefully use some of your time and motivate yourself.

Sometimes remembering what you used to enjoy doing as a child can link you back into the ideal work for you.

I, for instance, from a very young age would sit all my teddies and dolls in a circle and would hand out exercise books to them. I would play for hours pretending I was teaching them.

When I was in my late teens and early 20s, it never occurred to me to go into the teaching profession. I had lost sight of my true path in the noise and confusion of everyone around me controlling my choices and being influenced by other people's advice. It wasn't until I was at the Hackney Careers Office (see Chapter 1) talking to unemployed young people that I got connected to my passion for making a difference. That's when I decided I would study to become an English Literature teacher, which eventually led me to the work I do now.

Over to you

Back to childhood

Before we journey back to childhood, read and reflect on these questions.

- Are you excited about getting up in the morning and facing your day?
- Is this the best thing you could be doing with your time?
- Are you living some of your values every day?
- Who benefits day to day from what you do?

Now we are ready to suspend our day-to-day life and head back to a time of fun and innocence when anything was possible.

Below, list some of the activities and games you enjoyed playing as a child.
- Childhood play memories:
- Where did you like to play?
- Who were you in the game?
- How did you feel?
- What else do you notice?

Take some time to be present in these memories. Next, reflect and consider how what you loved doing as a child is mirrored in what you do now or would love to do. Fascinating isn't it? You are now getting closer to your purpose.

I need to get back to the ocean

During one of my retreats in California, I had taken a group of CEOs through a variety of processes to ascertain deeper levels of meaning and purpose in their life. The final one was where I asked them to present to the group their vision boards (Chapter 6) for their future life. One participant whose name was Jose, a senior executive in a global management consulting practice, was presenting his vision board and had not noticed that all his images were depicting ocean scenes. I asked him at that point what he had most enjoyed doing as a child.

With no hesitation, he said 'being by the ocean and surfing'.

When I asked him how often he gets to do that now, his whole face crumpled, and he said he was too busy in the office running projects so he never had the time to practise like he did as a teenager. On further examination we managed to surface that at the ocean he felt alive, full of his vital energy force, he was happy, carefree and fulfilled.

He realized that he had completely forgotten the environment he needed to flourish and be happy. Instead, he was doing a job that paid well and gave him a lot of status, but due to the long hours he had neglected his wife and his marriage had hit rock bottom. To escape from this treadmill, he was having affairs. He was neither happy nor satisfied.

After the retreat, he wrote to me to tell me that he has given up smoking, stopped the affairs and is now mentoring and coaching young under-privileged boys to surf on Sunday mornings. He had gone back to the ocean, and he is making a contribution.

He did not even have to leave his job; he just had to find a space in his week where he could connect to his highest self and nourish his soul. In his case, it was teaching kids to surf on a Sunday morning at the ocean.

Letting go of control

In order to connect more regularly to your highest self and inner wisdom, you must let go of the need to be constantly in control, rational, logical and in your head and enter the heart space so that you can loosen the mind thought control and surrender to a flow of energy that comes from the heart.

Trusting in your highest self will allow you to go with the flow of life, allowing your inner wisdom to articulate your calling.

Once you have defined your overall direction coming from your core values as your compass, you can let go of over-controlling your life. The appropriate wind will fill your sails and speed you in the right direction.

ROUTINES AND RITUALS KEEP US ON THE PATH

The most purposeful people I know all seem to have clear disciplines and rituals. If they are fit, they tend to have a regular gym routine, run or some other regular physical activity. If they are happily married, they tend to spend quality time with their families. If they are calm, they regularly do yoga or meditate every day. If they are muscle bound, they obviously do a lot of weight training. The truth will out from every pore!

> Anything you have achieved in life has come about through a regular commitment.

It's no surprise that regular routines and rituals can keep us on our chosen path. Later in the book, I will be going into more detail about how you can best look after yourself so that you can stay motivated, purposeful and on your path. However, you have a bit of reading and contemplating to do before we get to that!

My biggest recommendation for you at this stage of the journey is to create a space in your busy week to read this book, journal and do the exercises. Make maximum use of the guidance in these pages; in order to give yourself the best chance at having insights, you only need a journal (iPad or whatever you like to use) and space.

 Over to you

Create your space for purposeful contemplation

Find an area in your home where you feel calm and peaceful. This space should be away from the hustle and bustle of the general household. It's a space where you can be with yourself uninterrupted. Many men I know like to escape to 'their cave'. This could be an outbuilding or their study. The important thing is that you can escape into your own little haven. Here you can connect with yourself and begin your journalling routine.

Whenever I run my retreats and workshops, I always send an 'ideal room set' up request to the client or hotel banqueting manager before I arrive. Even though they may have set up the room with a circle of chairs as opposed to a formal boardroom style, I may need to spend a good hour and sometimes more really 'creating the space'. When people enter, I like them to feel something special is going to happen.

Space will respond to the love and care you put into it. Have you ever laid a table in preparation for a special event, a romantic supper or dinner party? You put flowers on the table, light some candles and make sure the space is just right. You are investing time and attention to detail because you are coming from a loving, caring energy. You obviously care about your guests.

> This is how you should treat yourself. It is essential that throughout this journey you create some space for yourself so that you can spend quality time and get the most out of this book.

- Write down somewhere you can go in your house away from noise and interruptions.
- Consider ways you can connect with yourself when you are calm and feeling resourced and at the same time take care of your spiritual well-being.

Whatever activity or space helps you to connect to your highest self is appropriate. It does not have to look a certain way; it's an individual choice, e.g., it could be your car. You may need to experiment with a number of different places until you find one that suits you. Currently, you may be unconsciously doing certain things that feed you spiritually, but you haven't as yet become conscious of them. Consider for a moment what they might be.

Congratulations – you are now one step closer to your purpose. You understand the difference between head and heart. You have explored childhood play memories, which will have triggered something powerful within you. Next it's time to reflect in your space. Spend some time writing and reflecting. Notice what comes up and how you feel.

Key thinking points

- What did you think your purpose was when you started this chapter?
- How has it developed now that you have allowed childhood memories to come in?
- What will you do right now to create your space, so that you can get connected to your purpose?
- What is your purpose and how will you, would you like to, express it?

Practise this daily mantra

'I am living and sharing my purpose from my highest self.'

PART TWO

Free Yourself: What Gets in the Way of Your Happiness?

3

We All Have a RAT

'*What we achieve inwardly will change outer reality.*'

Plutarch

The interesting thing about this journey is that as we find ourselves, as we did in Part One, voices for our limitations come creeping in. Imagine now that you understand these and why they appear, and that you have a set of tools that will enable you to quiet them.

Your next challenge is to begin to understand how your mind works so that you can develop and motivate yourself to create the life you want. Part of that is expressing a more passionate and positive you.

Becoming conscious of your state of mind is the first step to self-awareness. Many people I come across have huge egos. The ego self wants to be right and uses a lot of energy to protect itself.

When everything in life is going well, and we are going through normal, familiar and comfortable experiences, it is quite difficult to distinguish your authentic self from your ego self. However, as soon as you experience challenges, difficulties or people who are blocking you from what you want to do or are telling you how to do things, these become like a red rag to a bull. Being in these circumstances activates our survival instincts.

During my workshops, if I want people to learn new ideas and operate in different ways, I know sooner or later I shall be asking them to leave their comfort zones. When anyone is being asked to leave their comfort zone, this is when they tend to tune into a voice. 'A voice?' I hear you say. Yes, that voice. The voice that is a running commentary in your head. The one that goes something like this … '*Oh no, I am going to have to read aloud, or share my feelings in a room full of strangers, oh no perhaps I will need to get up and go on stage yikes …* ' and then the voice that gives you lots of suggestions to get you out of this uncomfortable situation. '*Maybe you should go to the loo and avoid having to talk, look away so you won't be asked.*' Sound familiar?

MEET YOUR RAT

This is a good time to introduce you to a little character that will feature in this chapter.

RATional Mind

Imagine a very large RAT. Yes, I said RAT – imagine the whiskers and the long, pinky, thick tail. Now imagine it gnawing away at your thoughts, your dreams, your best-laid plans.

Gnawing away at everything and anything. This RAT is my metaphor for **RATIONAL MIND.** The rational mind has one main role in life, and that is to keep you safe or, to put it a better way, keep you surviving. The primary driver and agenda for the RATional mind is – **YOUR SURVIVAL.** If life presents us with a risky choice, this RAT gets very loud in our heads and begins to chatter away to us at a million miles an hour, normally arguing for our limitations.

Your RATTY tape recordings

I want you to imagine your RAT sitting in your brain between your eyes. Like a secret video camera, it captures on tape every experience you have ever had in life that made a deep impression on you.

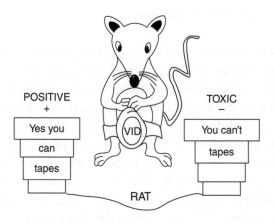

The RAT sits in the middle of two piles of videotapes. The pile on the right is everything in life you did badly, where you failed, screwed up, hurt yourself, or looked stupid. I'll call these 'toxic trauma tapes'.

On the left, RAT has a pile of tapes of you being great, successful winning and achieving. I'll call these your 'big you up
tapes'.

The toxic trauma tapes

Every time life presents you with similar, undesirable circumstances; RAT replays that toxic tape, and you automatically relive all the feelings, emotions and physical sensations.
The toxic trauma tapes stored on the right are very deeply
recorded in your memory banks and these tapes are very difficult to erase. RAT's intention is to keep you safe and stop
you from repeating the same mistake that historically caused
you pain or embarrassment. To make the message even more
powerful, RAT is simultaneously giving you a stream of negative and limiting self-talk to stop you in your tracks and cause
you to make a different decision. Decisions that will keep you
in your comfort zone and safe.

For instance, let us say that you were poor at reading as a
child and now as an adult you have been given an opportunity
to make a presentation to a group of people from a stage. At
this point RAT pulls out the tape of you at school when things
did not go well for you. RAT wants to remind you of all the
thoughts and feelings you had back then by way of stopping
you going through the same negative experience. RAT may
begin to give you reasons why you should not do this: '*You
can't stand up on stage and present to this large group of people, are you mad? Do you remember the last time you were
asked to do that by your teacher at school and you made a real
fool of yourself and fluffed all your words?*' At this stage, you
may even start sweating, and feel hot under the collar as RAT
replays for you all the sensations you had back in your childhood when you were last asked to stand on a stage. This is

an outdated survival strategy that does not serve you in your adult life, and it is imperative that you see it for what it is.

The 'big you up' tapes

On the other hand, we must remember that RAT also has a pile tapes on the left-hand side. These are all the experiences where you looked cool; you were winning, tapes of past experiences where you were successful. Those of us who have had a life of positive and good experiences have an easier time, as RAT will replay encouraging self-talk. For example: *'Yes go ahead and ski off that black run, you are really good at sport – remember the time you did a similar thing on that school trip and you won the school ski race?'* On these occasions RAT can be your best friend, encouraging you to take a risk based on past (positive) experience.

Getting out of the toxic RAT zone

Many of the people I meet have all sorts of fears and phobias, and if they listened to their RAT they would never put a foot out of their comfort zone.

According to Daniel Goleman, in his 1996 book *Emotional Intelligence*, we are constantly scanning our environment looking for threats. To be precise, the amygdala (an almond-shaped part of the limbic brain), is standing guard like an emotional sentinel, challenging every situation, every perception, with one question in mind, the most primitive: IS THIS A THREAT TO MY SURVIVAL? Is this something I should fear? If we get a YES, the amygdala reacts instantaneously and triggers our fight, fright or flight response. The amygdala – RAT if you will – pulls the adrenalin lever, sounds the alarm, and our entire system prepares for the onslaught of the perceived attack and gets ready for survival.

I have found over the years that this metaphor of RAT is a great working model for people to better understand how they keep themselves stuck in their comfort zones. This is especially true when they are learning new concepts and being invited to examine deeply held beliefs that do not serve them anymore, or are being asked to take a risk. During these occasions, we can become attached to our internal commentary.

'My sense of family duty was holding me back' – George

George's marriage was on the rocks due to the long separations caused by his crippling international travel schedule. He only saw his kids in the holidays, and his weight and health were spiralling out of control. Something had to give.

He yearned to hand over the reins of the family business to his younger brother so he could get on and live the life he had always wanted, but his strong sense of family duty and troubled relationship with his father were holding him back.

Although George was in his early 40s, he always felt intimidated and like a little boy in the presence of his father. Every time he got ready to bring up the subject he had visions of his father getting upset and stressed. A stream of RAT's disempowering thoughts would run through his mind: '*How could you possibly be so ungrateful and throw this privileged position back in your father's face, do you want to give him a heart attack? How can you let everybody down like this, think of your family! You are the eldest, and it's your duty as a good son … blah blah blah … '* coupled with '*Will I survive? Will my father's health suffer if I cause him this stress and upset? Will the family be OK or will they feel I have abandoned them for my selfish reasons?*'

During one of our sessions, I assisted George to articulate the voices and, therefore, become more conscious of them. Through this method, George learned that these voices were not coming from him, but from RAT, whose motive was to keep him in his comfort zone and stop him from rocking the boat. RAT was desperately trying to preserve the status quo and keep George safe. Eventually, having had time to reflect, George realized that he was now willing to take the risk and speak from his heart. In other words, to connect and express what HE wanted.

He spoke to his father at the very next opportunity. He was astonished at how receptive his father was and that he just wanted George to be happy. Had George continued to listen to his negative RAT voices, he may have been stuck in his 'I can't' world for some time. Trapped in his RATTY thoughts, paralysed by fear and negative self-talk.

As a result of taking the plunge, George now enjoys a stable home life. He has relocated to London with his family, joined a gym, and everyone is happy to be reunited. Things are working, and his marriage is on the mend.

FEAR AND EXCITEMENT ARE ONE AND THE SAME

Fight, fright or flight sensations, as they are sometimes called, occur when RAT picks up on threatening danger signals:

- A physical threat; for example, we are about to be mugged, or we are about to crash the car.
- A mental threat; for example, someone is saying NO to us when we are trying to get our way.

Over to you

Ask yourself

What physical sensations do you get when you experience danger and feel the fear? Tick all that apply:

- hot
- sweaty
- churning tummy
- shallow breathing
- moist hands
- dry mouth.

Next, consider the physical sensations of sheer excitement. Tick all that apply:

- hot
- sweaty
- churning tummy
- shallow breathing
- moist hands
- dry mouth

Guess what? They are all the same.

In other words, adrenaline being pumped through the body always creates the same physical sensations. However, RAT puts the experience through different software. When RAT wants to get us out of a dangerous situation, when our very survival is at stake, RAT pulls on the adrenalin lever and gives us all the physical sensations listed above. Not only that, he adds in some very powerful instructions: *'This is scary let's get you the hell out of here, run for your life!'*

But if RAT feels there is no danger presented, and indeed this is an exciting and enjoyable experience – like driving a fast car, a roller coaster ride, great sex, skiing down a black run – RAT creates the physical experience (we only have one kind of adrenaline) and sends you positive messages. '*This is exciting; you can enjoy this. When was the last time you felt this? Life is super, full of adrenaline and vitality, this is great, my heart is thumping … this is so exciting.*'

Regardless of whether there is a positive or negative experience, RAT is a very powerful advisor. With every experience, the physical sensations are the same. It's pure adrenaline rushing through your body. The only thing that's different is the tape RAT is playing for you. Clever RAT can convince you that black is white and white is black depending on the circumstances you find yourself in. RAT is very efficient at keeping you conscious of anything that threatens your survival.

Where does all this wiring come from?

When our ancestors were confronted with a threat to their survival in the form of a grizzly bear, tiger, or some other salivating beast, it was appropriate to sound the alarm, sending messages that enabled us to survive the imminent threat.

We do not come across many sabre-toothed tigers in the boardroom (though it may seem like it …), but our responses to any perceived threat to our survival are still there. **We are hard wired to survive.** However, we are over-surviving, and it's causing many people a lot of stress.

It is sometimes difficult to distinguish between real, close and present danger and a threat to our ego. Like our ancestors, most of us are scanning our environment for threats. As we do, we respond to this by going into over-survival mode and it becomes as if our very life is being threatened. Everyone's threshold for fear and pain is different; some people find simply walking into a room where there are people they don't know threatening. Social situations can make some people feel very uncomfortable, and their RAT can get very loud at these times. Others of us may find boardroom meetings scary. This is not only stressful but renders us powerless to see the real opportunities life has to offer us.

If we hit a barrier, for instance let's say we find out we have made a serious error at work which in turn has a knock on effect on everyone else in the department, the situation could be perceived by RAT as a life or death situation. In order to keep you safe, RAT plays a tape of your experiences – from the 'I do not want to repeat this' pile – that puts you back in an experience of fear. This, in turn, triggers the physical sensations of fight, fright or flight. This physical experience is coupled with negative and disempowering thoughts.

WE ALL HIT BARRIERS

I want you to remember a time when you were going about your day-to-day life feeling quite happy and suddenly you got an awful phone call, entered into a difficult conversation/argument, or even worse found out a loved one was ill or in trouble. In other words, metaphorically speaking, you hit a big brick wall. Keep this scenario in mind as you read the rest of this chapter.

When your scenario occurred, you probably had a physical reaction to the bad news. Plus you will have hit some negative emotional 'barriers'. Make a note of what these feelings typically are for you, and then consider the five key negative emotional barriers that I am going to introduce you to.

Five key negative emotional barriers

There are so many negative emotions you might hit, but to keep this simple I have distilled them into five key negative emotions: apathy, grief, fear, anger and pride.

Keep your scenario in mind and let's go on a journey. Remember, we are all different. Depending on your past experiences to date, and the emotional barrier you hit, you will experience the same situation differently to someone else.

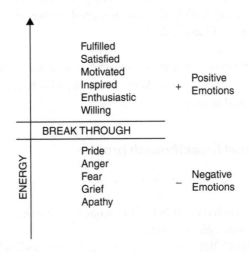

Let's explore each in turn:

- **APATHY** – this is one of the lowest human emotional states. The physiology of this state is low to no energy, slumped in the chair or lying down. Your RATional thoughts might be: *'What's the point? I can't be bothered with this anymore. I have failed. I am worthless! I have let everyone down.'*

- **GRIEF** – this is a slightly higher energy level and in this state we might have thoughts like: *'It's not fair, will it be OK, why me, why is this always happening to me?'*
- **FEAR** – in this state our energy is held in our stomachs, we can lose our appetite, and our thoughts might be: *'Will I survive, what if I lose my business, what if everybody wants out!'*
- **ANGER** – this is a much higher energy state and in this negative emotional state we're having frightful thoughts like *'I will kill them, I am furious!'* We pace up and down, as we feel so full of explosive negative energy.
- This energy can then turn in on itself and become **PRIDE**. This is the highest energy state of all the negative emotions, and is broadly an expression of **'I CAN'T'** and **'I WON'T'**: *'How dare they, who do they think they are/do they know who they are dealing with here, I am not apologizing, they are in the wrong, and I am right.'*

Nothing positive happens in these energy states. RAT thoughts that are negative keep us stuck, which in turn affects our emotional states.

Motivational breakthrough process

There are four stages to this model:

1. Once you have **IDENTIFIED** what your barriers are you can break through this cycle.
2. You **DECODE** your thoughts and feelings and acknowledge that you are trapped.
3. You focus on a **SHORT-TERM GOAL** (e.g. if you are in APATHY in bed you focus on getting up and going to the shower).
4. You **raise your energy** and **TRANSFORM** the RAT negative self-talk to positive self-talk, e.g. *'I can get through this I have done it before and will do again.'* Remind yourself that this too shall pass.

Take a look at the following diagram. You will be using this to 'break through' your RATTY tapes.

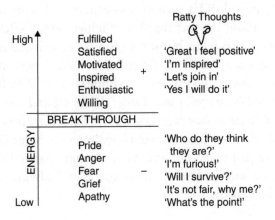

Once you have learned the motivational breakthrough method, you will move into a positive arena. You will have raised your energy, focused on a short-term goal and transformed your negative self-talk. You will notice that you are experiencing more positive emotions. As you transform your thoughts, you transform your emotions. Your physiology and focus are more positive; you are walking tall, smiling and expressing energy. You are now in the positive emotions of 'I can' and 'I will'. This is a wonderful space to be in and, once there, you will want to stay there.

You can hit any one of these negative barriers throughout the day. Your skill at managing the RAT voice in your head and your willingness to express energy and focus on a small, short-term goal will assist you to move through these states quickly and not dwell and wallow in a self-limiting stream of thoughts.

DON'T BE FOOLED BY YOUR FEELINGS

I remember when I worked for a big consulting practice. In the early days I did a stint as a salesperson. I remember feeling great about the fact that I was achieving my sales targets. However, I also felt a bit of a victim because I was not being given the salary increase I felt I deserved. I was in GRIEF about it, if you will. I was having thoughts like *'Why have they not noticed how well I am doing? It's not fair I am so much more productive than everyone else. Where is my bonus?'* One day, I plucked up the courage to walk to the Sales Director's office and just come out and ask for what I knew I deserved. Her office had a glass front so you could always see what mood she was in.

As I walked closer and closer, my RAT got louder and louder, 'What if she gets angry and throws me out? Who am I to ask for a salary increase? Am I that good? What if this just isn't the right time?' I could feel my heart thumping and my hands getting moist. Then I hit PRIDE: 'If she has not realized I deserve one then who am I to tell her? She should be coming to me!' With that, I turned around and started walking back to my office. Gradually the thumping subsided, my RAT went quiet. I sat down and congratulated myself on making the right decision. Which made me feel so much better. But had I done the right thing?

Just because you feel comfortable does not mean it's the right decision. Later, I found out that had I stepped out of my comfort zone, my Sales Director would have rewarded me with my inevitable rise six months earlier. In fact, she told me *'If you had come out and just asked me for a rise, I would have been compelled to give it to you as your results were so good.'*

Over to you

Time to break through

Go back to the scenario you chose earlier and add any other situations that you want to work on. Using the above list of barriers, identify which ones you typically go through. Apathy, grief, fear, anger or pride?

- Which emotional barriers do you typically hit?
- What thoughts are you having when you are in this emotional state?
- What happens just before – what is the trigger?
- Now go through all the negative emotions and try to articulate how you feel and what you are thinking in these states.
- What patterns are emerging?

Identify the barrier

PRIDE
    Feelings _____
    Thoughts _____
ANGER
    Feelings _____
    Thoughts _____
FEAR
    Feelings _____
    Thoughts _____
GRIEF
    Feelings _____
    Thoughts _____
APATHY
    Feelings _____
    Thoughts _____

Remember: being conscious of the voice in your head better equips you to control of it.

YOU ARE NOT YOUR RAT

I CAN	I WILL
I CAN'T	I WON'T

YOU ARE NOT YOUR RAT – it's just outmoded conditioning.

It's very important that you know when you are below the breakthrough line in your thoughts and emotions. Surface the voice and remember it is just a voice that you can choose to change.

Becoming aware of which state you are in at any moment is the first key to shifting your energy and state. You can either be:

- above the breakthrough line, feeling resourceful and positive, i.e. coming from a stance of 'I can' and 'I will'; or
- below the breakthrough line, in the negative, adopting a stance of 'I can't' and 'I won't'.

Taking responsibility

TAKING RESPONSIBILITY

Responsible Stance	Victim Stance
Chooses their response eg. When it rains they get an umbrella	Does not experience having choices – 'It's not fair!'

At any moment, you may see yourself as a victim of your circumstances and blame others for the situation you find yourself in. You say, '*Why me? It's not fair? Someone is to blame for this.*'

In this victim state you are experiencing separateness, dramatizing the story in your head, possibly even crying. In this state, you believe that life is doing this to you. You experience yourself as disempowered.

On the other side of the line, you could take responsibility for your circumstances. You could be above the line and feeling resourceful. You could be thinking '*What can I do about this? What are my options? How can I solve this issue?*' In this stance, you are choosing a better response to the circumstances you find yourself in.

'I was frustrated by my father's rules' – Sam

Working in a family business is never easy. Sam's father had many rules, one of which was that only family members could become directors.

Working with Sam was Ayesha, his sales manager. Ayesha worked hard and was a dedicated, loyal and productive member of staff. However, she frustrated him. Ayesha always seemed to want commission for the great sales her department was bringing in. Sam could not always give Ayesha what he knew she deserved. When he was faced with what he perceived as her demands, which he was helpless to deliver, he would routinely hit the negative emotion PRIDE. '*Who does she think she is, she is not the boss, she can't dictate to me how to run the company and make demands!*'

Once he had discussed this scenario with me and had the time to decode himself, he realized that his reaction was not directed at Ayesha but at his father and his rules.

Sam realized in his heart of hearts that his sales manager, Ayesha, should be promoted to director level as she was excel-lent at her job and a real company asset.

He realized his PRIDE was being triggered. What he needed to do was to face his father and let him know that he was mature enough now to make important business decisions. Having been fully able to decode his triggers, emotions and thoughts he was able to raise his energy and finally confront his father about the ridiculous rule. He persuaded his father, who was in his 80s, to see sense.

 Over to you

Decode your RAT brain

In this exercise, you will be decoding your emotional barriers. What we are doing is enabling you to raise your self-awareness so that you can pay attention to cues and patterns.

Go back to some of the typical routine scenarios that trigger you into the 'I can't and I won't' state. If you haven't written them in your journal, do so now; if you have, review them. Notice what categories they fall into. Remember to make a note of what was happening in the lead-up, how you reacted and what happened next.

Over to you

Set a short-term goal

Just as Sam did in the story above, consider your scenarios and ask: 'What short term goal could I set that will take me from the barrier, through the breakthrough line, into participation, motivation and creativity ('I can and I will')?'

Moving you forward and raising your energy

Next we want to motivate you towards satisfaction. Using your list of scenarios, and the table below, list the trigger and the emotion you feel. Take each scenario all the way through to impact. For example:

Trigger – criticism from the boss about job performance.
Emotion – anger at boss and frustration with self.
Thought – who does he think he is speaking to me like that?
Behaviour – sulk and tell others that the boss is not up to the job.
Impact – spiral of negative thoughts and worsening performance.

Trigger	Emotion	Thought	Behaviour	Impact

BENEFITS OF RECODING YOUR RAT

Now that you have raised your awareness of your inner RAT, coupled with becoming conscious of the emotional barriers you hit – apathy, grief, fear, anger or pride – you can benefit from exercising the discipline of decoding your thoughts and feelings and using the motivational breakthrough method to change your behaviour. Using this method means that, as you recognize how all of your triggers create a chain reaction, you can put in place actions that will enable you to DECODE and RECODE in a fraction of a second. The net result is that you will have made a choice to react differently. As you react differently, physically, emotionally and spiritually, you will motivate yourself into a better state. When you then release feel-good hormones, you will create new neural pathways, which become your norms for the future.

Congratulate yourself for being able to identify, decode, set goals, raise your energy and transform your RATTY thoughts quickly and effectively. Next we shall be surfacing the many RATs that might be causing havoc so that these too can be quelled.

Key thinking points

- Your RAT is interested in having you survive and keeping you in your comfort zone.
- Your RAT will feed you messages that will convince you to argue for your limitations.
- When you hit a barrier, i.e. apathy, grief, fear, anger or pride, use the motivational breakthrough process to move you above the line.
- Be sure to check off thoughts and feelings, thank your RAT for sharing, raise your energy, focus on a short-term goal and recode yourself.

Practise this daily mantra

'I am not my RAT.'

4

Saboteur RATs Are Running Amok

··

'Make sure your worst enemy doesn't live between your own ears.'

Laird Hamilton

You've been introduced to your RAT, and you are now aware that you are not your RAT. You have established that at any time RAT can be your best friend, encouraging you to go for it. At other times, however, RAT is your worst enemy, trying to sabotage and stop you from having the life you want and keeping you from taking the risks you would like to take. In other words, keeping you wrapped up safely in your comfort zone.

Your cheerleader RAT (who you will meet later) is often drowned out by the multitude of other saboteur RATTY voices in your heads. In other words, we have a number of RAT voices nagging at us; they all have a slightly different message, opinion and character. In this chapter, I will define more clearly for you some of the typical RAT voices and how you can be aware of them so you can manage them better.

Giving each of these RAT voices a character and name and thus personifying them is very helpful. Once we can recognize these saboteurs of our otherwise confident selves, we have more awareness and control over them. The more conscious you are of them, the better equipped you will be to manage and keep them at bay. When you begin your motivational life planning, I assure you they are likely to show up.

The moment you venture into the unknown area of personal development and begin to shine a light into all the areas you want to change, sure enough the saboteur RAT voices will show up and try to undermine any attempt on your part to take a risk or leave your comfort zone. That's when you need to be on guard and on the look out to stop them in their tracks!

WHERE DO THESE OTHER RAT VOICES COME FROM?

Depending on the way you were raised, you may motivate yourself in a number of different ways. Fundamentally speaking, we all want to be safe, secure and have a sense of belonging. You may be familiar with Maslow's hierarchy of needs, which shows that these are some of the most basic human needs. They must be addressed on our way to self-actualization.

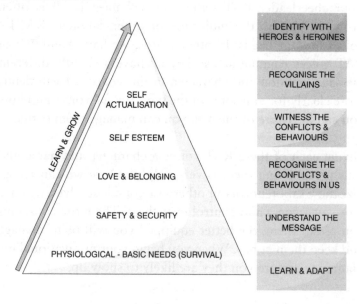

In 1974, Kahler and Caper wrote an essay studying human behaviour patterns. They held that much of our behaviour is modelled on one of our parents. They discovered that the conversations, phrases and advice we heard in our households, specifically from our parents over and over again, became 'mini scripts' in our heads. For instance, if you heard your mother or father every morning utter that immortal phrase 'Hurry up you'll be late for school!' it may have become a habitual mind thought, which turned into an unconscious behaviour.

When we are under stress, these 'mini scripts' or 'drivers' become subconscious attempts by us to behave in ways that will gain us the recognition we need from others; they are also programmed responses to the messages we carry in our heads from important people from the past (Hay 2009: p. 96). These can be distilled into five key behaviour drivers.

1. Be perfect

This script tells you that nothing but complete perfection will do. Everything must be right, first time. Any criticism is taken very badly and out of proportion and sets off a cascade of other undermining beliefs about not being good enough. If you recognize this aspect in yourself, you will also know that you are known for your accuracy, organization and reliability. Conversely, you may deliver late, as you have to check all of the details and may actually include too many details.

2. Hurry up

This script urges you to do everything in double time. This is like being high on caffeine or other substances. People who suffer from this inner commentary find it hard to listen to slow-paced people and do not give others time to finish their sentences. They already know what they are going to say.

Deadlines are often missed as they cram too much into their day. People with these tendencies work quickly and try to get a lot done in a short time frame. You may enjoy having many projects on the go; however, in your haste to over deliver, you may miss details and not actually start until the deadline is looming.

3. Please people

This script makes sure that everyone you meet likes you. You enjoy being in company and always show an interest in others. You do things for other people without asking, seek to create harmony and are intuitive. However, you must agree, conform and on no occasion confront or tell people the truth about how you are really feeling as you risk being disliked or rejected.

4. Be strong

This script tells you to just get on with it! You are usually calm under pressure and love to have a project to tackle that is on a tight deadline. However, you put yourself and your energy at risk as you adopt what the British call a stiff upper lip. You do not ask for help as you are strong and can do things on your own. Expressing vulnerability is needy, and you do not want to be pitied or seen as a victim. You end up becoming overloaded and resentful.

5. Try hard

This script encourages you to try hard; it's all about effort but rarely looks at what it will take to achieve the result. You approach tasks with great enthusiasm and love new projects. However, you tend to expend lots of energy without necessarily getting the result. You are an ideas person, rather than a follow-through person, and it can sometimes seem as if you are self-sabotaging.

MODELLING OUR PARENTS' BEHAVIOUR

Children grow up rapidly and learn a lot of information about how to walk, talk, eat, stay safe, not get into trouble, get love, food, warmth and so on. Our parents or primary carers guide much of this early behaviour. We had baby RATs helping us to survive every day, and who better to model ourselves on than our parents – who at that time were the all-seeing, all-powerful centres of our universe – they could do no wrong and provided us with our every need.

As you begin to mature and develop your own personality, you begin to take in how your parents communicate and which one gets their way most of the time. You very rapidly work out who seems to be the boss, who is happier and more fulfilled.

Let's assume dad was dominant but mum got her way by being 'nice' and gentle; the child may adopt that style of behaviour and therefore also inherit the 'people pleaser' script that goes with it.

However, if the child saw dad getting more of what he wanted around the house by being a bit of a bully, then the child would be likely to adopt similar behaviour patterns. Remember: we all have a stake in our own survival and our parents were no different. We saw them 'surviving' certain difficult situations and depending on the behaviour they adopted to keep themselves safe, and thus we learned to do the same.

Over to you

What was the typical behaviour of your significant carers?

Make a note of your primary carers and significant adults, then jot down their typical behaviour while thinking about the five drivers. At this stage, you do not need to segment them, merely observe whether they fit into one or several of the drivers.

Can you identify their behaviour patterns?

Next, review what you have written and see if you can identify one or more of the five drivers. It might be helpful to use coloured pens to highlight each one. Once you have done this, grab a cuppa or take a ten-minute walk break. When you get back, read and review.

Significant phrases

Next, pull out any significant phrases that they used. Make a list. Are any of those phrases yours? Then consider how these impact on your behaviour and how that makes you feel.

Who is your model?

You will no doubt see a pattern forming. Review what you have written and decide who you have been modelling yourself on. Consider this from two angles: you as a child and you as an adult.

Next, put yourself into a number of scenarios – work, home and social – who shows up? Then extend that to your wider community: think of partners, your children, friends and acquaintances.

Imagine your authentic self

When you consider all of these ways of behaving you will, I am sure, be cringing; I know I did when I first realized. It was in that realization that I knew there was another way. My question to you, as it was to myself, is: What would happen if you dropped the behaviour and acted more like your authentic self?

LEARNT SURVIVAL BEHAVIOUR

A number of the men I work with were sent to a private boarding school, some of them went when they were as young as 7 years old. *'Be strong, little boys don't cry, stiff upper lip'*, was common feedback while growing up. Imagine being faced with staying in a boarding school with often no hope of seeing their parents until exeat. This meant that they had to learn to survive, how to self-soothe and get on with it. Enter the RAT teaching them at an early age how to survive and get through. Many of them learned how to suppress their feelings, emotions and tears and just get on with it.

Later on in life, these drivers may show up as not being very tolerant of emotional people. Not being willing to disclose or unable to open up easily to people. It's hardly surprising that a number of them find it very tough to connect and talk about emotions – it's the way they were raised!

'I realized I'd never told my daughter "I love you"' – Dan

Dan went to boarding school when he was 7. His father was in the army and moved around a lot, being an only child his parents thought he would be much happier with the stability of an English boarding school. He saw his parents in the holidays but would always spend exeat weekends at friends' houses as his parents were abroad. He was envious of the happy family atmosphere he witnessed at his friends' houses. The informal atmosphere, warmth and physical affection were given with so much ease, whereas Dan had a formal relationship with both his parents.

At the workshop Dan attended, we were discussing values. Love was a common theme for this group. 'Love is a primary value for many people. How do you express love?' I asked. Other people in the room were sharing how they tell their kids every day, at the end of every phone call how much they love them. Suddenly Dan went very quiet and seemed to be having trouble breathing.

'I have never told my daughter "I love you".'

This was the first time he understood that his parenting style was just like his father's: formal and very matter of fact. Tears started rolling down his face; it was as if a curtain had been lifted. I asked him to take the opportunity for some time out to write a letter to his daughter telling her what she meant to him and how much he loved her. It was important he do it there and then before the saboteur RATs put him off the idea!

A few weeks later, I had a message from Dan telling me that this one gesture had begun a process of healing with not only his daughter but also his wife. He had realized that feeling love was not enough; he had to demonstrate it and show it.

RATs SPEAK IN MANY TONGUES

RAT speaks to us in many tongues depending on the situation. When you were young, these scripts/voices may have been crutches you formulated to keep you safe. Like a computer, they run software that becomes who we (think we) are. However, as you mature, this software gets outdated and is no longer required. In fact, it can sabotage your best-laid plans. The voices generally argue for your limitations and, as you know, keep you in your comfort zone. These voices are RAT in different guises.

So, who are these RATTY fiends? They are a set of automatic and habitual mind triggers, each with its own message, opinion and character.

If you have never thought about them in this way – beware, as they may have become invisible inhabitants of your mind. We often are not aware they exist. This is what makes them particularly dangerous, especially when we are on automatic pilot and allow them to take over. They have been there since we were very young, we do not see them as saboteurs; on the contrary, we totally identify with them and feel that they are just part of who we are. Getting conscious and recognizing that we are not our RAT is the first stage to strengthening our authentic self.

Let's meet the RATs

Here is a list of the nine most common RAT voices with a brief description of how they undermine us. As you read through, make a note and see if you can recognize any of yours in the list.

1. The abusive RAT

ABUSIVE RAT

This voice is constantly shouting at you, letting you know that you are not good enough. Sneering at you, and calling you names ... '*Oh, you stupid idiot ... you forgot your keys ... you are so stupid you have missed the train again ... you always screw everything up!*'

You are not worthy of having this or that; you don't deserve to be happy and fulfilled. This voice puts you on a constant guilt trip about everything you do that you enjoy. '*Who are you to take time out for yourself you should work harder, try harder, don't be so lazy.*'

2. The critical RAT

CRITICAL RAT

Sometimes this voice is referred to as the inner critic, negative self-talk, the committee: this voice has all the reasons ready for why the plan is a stupid, dangerous, hopeless or otherwise ill-advised course of action. This invader is particularly adept at taking a small piece of the truth and fabricating a blanket reason for stopping or never starting. It is an expert in everything; mothering, cooking, driving, writing, anything we are doing this RAT knows better. '*If I were you, I would do it this way.*'

3. The 'poor me' victim RAT

VICTIM RAT

The victim RAT craves sympathy and needs constant love and attention. The victim needs recognition for the pain it has been through in life. It's all '*Woe is me!*' and can be very draining. When your victim shows up, most people want to run a mile as you can become a black hole of doom and gloom. It keeps us safe in the knowledge that any mistake or failure is the fault of someone else, our circumstances, or even the colour of the sky. This victim has taken up permanent residence in the I can't, I won't world. '*Why me?*' and '*it's not fair*' are its mantras.

4. The hurry up RAT

HURRY UP RAT

This is the hurry up voice in our heads, where everything must be done in double quick time and if not we are totally incompetent. It won't let us live in the moment and allow us to smell the roses, as it's too intent on getting us on to doing the next thing. When we tune in to this voice we are in great stress and constantly futuring to the moment when we can put our feet up at the end of the day. It's never right now.

5. The judgemental RAT

JUDGEMENTAL RAT

This RAT compels you to find fault with everything and everyone, especially with yourself, others and your circumstances. This voice has you thinking that without it you would move to your lowest common denominator and never achieve anything. This voice is tough love; we may even mistake it for a parental voice, which has our best interests at heart. Keeping us on the straight and narrow and nose to the grindstone. When you are under the power of this voice, you find yourself feeling judgemental and distanced from the people you are judging. After all, if they don't agree with you, why should you fraternize with them or be their friend? This voice definitely judges a book by its cover; if people are not speaking, saying, dressing or acting in a way that you find familiar and safe you may judge them.

6. The perfectionist RAT

BE PERFECT
RAT

This voice takes any detail or any blemish and amplifies it to the point of invalidating all the good stuff you have achieved. For instance, if 50 people fill out your evaluation praising you or your company for doing a great job, this voice will pick up on the one negative comment and amplify it out of all proportion. It will beat you up about it and put the negative comment centre stage, ignoring the other 49 that gave you high marks.

7. The 'please like me' or Mr Nice RAT

'PLEASE LIKE ME' RAT

This RAT voice has to have approval and acceptance from everyone. It's manipulating everyone to 'please like me', often using a smiley expression, being non-confrontational and wanting everyone to be dependent on them. This saboteur stops us from being direct and authentic in our communication. Saying no or giving direct feedback is impossible when this voice is around. It tells you that if you were to be direct or tell the whole truth, people would not like you.

8. The clever dick RAT

By
CLEVER DICK
RAT

Book
of Clever
Theories

This is the voice of reason, rationalizing and intellectualizing everything. This voice can be emotionally disconnected and is always coming from the head space not the heart space. It hides behind rationalizing the emotions and is never willing to disclose vulnerability. It shrouds us in an impenetrable suit of armour.

9. The be careful/fearful RAT

BE CAREFUL/FEARFUL RAT

The 'be careful' RAT is like a rabbit in the headlights constantly petrified about what might happen. It tells you to watch out for that car, makes you feel intense panic and anxiety about all the dangers surrounding you and what could go wrong. This voice projects failure and terrifying 'what if' scenarios to keep you from leaving your comfort zone. If we listen to this voice, we become cowardly and avoid doing anything that could put us into danger. This is one that can influence the parenting of young kids. Every command starts with *'be careful … you don't fall, be careful … don't run…'*.

Having these voices in our heads is a universal phenomenon. Becoming aware and specifically conscious of each and everyone of RAT's personality types will help you get control of them and stop being sucked into believing what they tell you.

Those of us who are not aware of all the guises of RAT are especially at risk. Being unconscious of them means they get to control you. All of us have a self-sabotaging inner voice – or voices – that holds us back. Preserving the status quo is part of these RAT voices' job. So it's no wonder that when we contemplate moving forward in a big way it wakes up the RATs; the bigger the challenge, the louder the RAT voices become.

The good news is you have positive voices too.

Your cheerleader RAT

This voice is your biggest fan and is truly on your side. This voice believes in you; this is the voice that picks you up when you are down and brushes you off. It's the voice that praises you when you have done a great job or managed to achieve something you were going for. It's the soothing, kind, self-loving voice that nurtures you and notices your natural gifts and talents. This represents your inner wisdom and is a pathway to getting more in touch with your 'highest self' (see Chapter 2).

Your cheerleader RAT voice sits in the frontal lobe part of the brain (neocortex). It's the more evolved and mature part of us. It's the part of the brain that enables humans to make meaning. The other RAT voices sit in the amygdala part of the brain, which is the most primitive part, and are interested in survival (fight, fright or flight behaviour).

The frontal, more evolved, part of the brain is the part of you that rises to the challenge at hand and let's you know you can do it; it tells you to '*go for it, knock em dead, don't forget to be awesome*'. It comes from the positive emotional space of 'I can' and 'I will'. Allowing you the freedom to explore with an open mind, the creative part of you has a willingness to participate in the wonderful challenges life presents us with. It's the part of you that wants to develop and grow and has a yearning for meaning and purpose. This is the part that encouraged you to pick up this book and will help you connect to your deeper values and purpose and ensure they are fully activated in your unfolding life from this point onwards.

 Over to you

Meeting your RATTY voices

Now that you have started to look at where your scripts might have come from, it's time to examine the RATTY voices that have crawled into your headspace over time.

Go back through the list of RAT voices and bring to mind some of your experiences.

Time to get creative

Feeling artistic? Let's get RAT onto paper. Grab a large sheet of paper and draw the faces of these saboteur rodents. It doesn't matter that you don't think you can draw; it's the fun of scribbling their wicked faces and features.

Next, name them, and bring them to life by giving them characteristics. Ask if they were a feeling or a colour, sound, or taste what would they be?

Getting conscious of the RAT voices

In order to get in control of these rodents, you need to be conscious of them. Ask yourself: When do these RATs show up? As you review your drawings, identify the thoughts and feelings you are having when they show up.

Thank your RATs

Yes, I do mean for you to say thank you. You might say to yourself: 'thank you victim RAT for sharing with me your insecurities, but I am going to do it anyway'. Acknowledging the voices and giving gratitude for the lesson is extremely powerful.

Decode and recode your RAT with the motivational breakthrough method

Use the motivation breakthrough method (see Chapter 3) of decoding your thoughts and feelings, raising your energy and focusing on a short-term goal. Transform your thoughts and tap into your highest self voice. Follow this process to say goodbye to RATTY chat and be connected to your cheerleader.

1. Choose a recent experience.
2. Tune into which RATTY voice is being activated, e.g. abusive, critical, poor me, hurry up, judgemental, etc.

3. Remember you are not your RAT.
4. Say thank you.
5. Remind yourself of the breakthrough model.
6. Identify your barrier(s).
7. Decode yourself (check feelings, thoughts and energy levels).
8. Focus on a short-term doable goal.
9. Tap into your cheerleader RAT.
10. Raise your energy, move and transform your thoughts to cheerleader ('I can' and 'I will' thoughts …).
11. Celebrate.

'I always put my family's needs before mine' – Reshma

Reshma was a kind, thoughtful, lovely lady who lived in Beirut. Having worked with her on a number of workshops, we were exploring what she wanted from her life over the next 5–10 years. During one of our sessions, I asked her to compile a collage of all the experiences she wanted in her life. She spent hours creating the most intricate vision board. There was an English countryside, beautiful houses on avenues flanked with trees. People walking dogs, images of people relaxing in the park and strolling along.

As I gazed at her, it struck me that none of these experiences were out of her reach. So I asked her, 'Reshma, do you have a dog?' She answered 'No'.

'Would you like to live in England?'

'Yes,' she said.

'So, what's stopping you?'

She became very tearful and began to explain that as a girl she always knew that being the eldest she had to be a good girl and look after her siblings. Her father was never around, so her mother was left with total responsibility most of the time. This was Reshma's way of pleasing her mother and getting her approval.

Even as she matured into a young woman, she married a man much older than her (whom she respected but never felt much passion for) in order to please her parents.

Now her life was about serving her family, being at the beck and call of her husband and daughters and nursing her dad, who had had a stroke.

So I asked her: When will you put your own needs first?

She said she had a longer term strategy, and as soon as her girls had all left to go to university she would be moving to the UK and getting a dog. She would spend her days walking in the parks and putting her own needs first.

I explained that she had been so busy trying to please everyone she had put her own life on hold and her own sense of fulfilment and satisfaction. Her girls were not going to thank her for that in the future. In short, she had become everyone's doormat.

Remember that every doormat has WELCOME written on it.

Reshma was playing out a story that she had in her head; she never thought to challenge her 'script' of the way her life was panning out.

I wonder if you can spot Reshma's dominant RAT? Yes, you guessed it, victim RAT.

HOW DO YOU DEFINE YOURSELF?

We are always meeting people in life who ask us about ourselves. As a quick elevator pitch, how do you describe yourself? Broadly speaking, do you talk about yourself as a victim or generally as a happy and successful person who is growing and learning? The way we talk about our life, how we remember events and also how we cast ourselves in the story is very significant. If your life were a film, would it be a drama, comedy or a tragedy? What is the lens you view your life through?

 Over to you

Change your script, change your life

By now you will know who you modelled yourself on, how their scripts influenced you, and have an understanding of what kind of scripts you run and what RATs you let run amok in your head. You will have used the breakthrough method to decode these, and now you are ready to change the scripts. Your mantra now is: change my scripts, change my life.

Your life as a story

1. Your life is a series of stories. If you were going to tell us about your life story, what would you say? Keep it short for now.
2. Draw a picture of you in your life, use a metaphor if you wish.
3. Who are you in the picture?
4. What role are you playing?

Current life script

With your picture in front of you, carry on writing your life story. Again keep it brief, one side of A4 will do. Take time to write out the highlights. Focus on some key events. Pay attention to the dramas and difficulties and how you got through. When you have finished, do something else for at least 10 minutes. Then come back to reflect.

Points to consider

1. How are you depicted in this story?
2. Winner, resourceful, or victim, loser?
3. How do you feel about yourself?
4. Where does it get you in life?

Future life script 1

Imagine that it is one year into the future. Rewrite the life script looking at yourself through a more empowered lens. Take time to rewrite your script from a different vantage point. In this story, you are cast as positive, resourceful, authentic and strong. You can use your imagination to depict yourself as your ideal best self. For example: '*I had a challenging childhood that taught me to be resilient and self-sufficient.*'

This is for your eyes only, so you can indulge yourself in any way you want. Go on, knock yourself out. It's great fun. Start writing now.

When you have finished, take your 10 minutes out and then come back to review.

Points to consider
1. How are you depicted in this future story? Winner? Resourceful?
2. How do you feel about yourself now?
3. How would you remember your life if you thought like this?
4. What will being like this and thinking like this get you in life?

YOU CAN REWRITE THE SCRIPT – TIME TO CUT THE UMBILICAL CORD

You already know that growing up you were open, wide-eyed and susceptible to all manner of influences. Your parents (assuming they were your primary carers) would have inadvertently given you their great traits, e.g. kindness and generosity, but also their weaknesses, e.g. whining about the price of everything.

Everything they said and did has had an impact on you, the experiences they provided you with, the way they parented, the words they used and habitual things they said. **Their map of the world became, at least when you were young, your map of the world.**

They were doing their best with the resources they had at the time.

Whether you love and approve of your parents or have a difficult and estranged relationship with them, you are what you are. You are the product of years and years of conditioning. Now you have an opportunity to tune into the conditioning and change it. You can choose a different response. A new inner script about how things were and are will really help you.

If you view your circumstances through the 'Woe is me lens' you will probably create more of the same. However, if you can – like the song in *Life of Brian* – always look on the bright side of life, you can rewrite the script, forgive and move on. Cut the cord and move on.

Congratulations! You have done some great work, identifying your RATs. In the next chapter, I will be giving you tools to rewire some of those limiting beliefs that have kept you stuck for years.

Key thinking points

1. RAT takes residence from an early age and is influenced by your significant carers.
2. RATs have voices and scripts that become a part of you.
3. You are not your RAT.
4. You can change your RATTY chat.
5. When you have decoded and rewritten your RATTY chat, your motivation and energy for life will skyrocket.
6. What has to happen so that you want to change your RATTY chat and scripts?

Practise this daily mantra

'Change my script, change my life.'

Wired for Satisfaction

'Whether you think you can, or you think you can't –
you're right.'

Henry Ford

With every thought, and every decision we make about ourselves, we seal our fate.

We are authors of our universe: what we think we are, we project out into the world. We are responsible for our thoughts and their outcomes.

Awareness of this fact is the most important stage of personal transformation. Becoming conscious of your limiting thinking patterns that have prevented you from living your life at the optimum levels of success and fulfilment is the next challenge. Most of the negative beliefs we have about ourselves are largely based on some erroneous evidence we gathered back in our childhood. If we never dismantle these entrenched beliefs, they can control the views we have of ourselves; which in turn show up as limitations later on in life and become self-fulfilling prophecies. For example:

- I'm no good at relationships.
- I can't lose weight.
- I am not pretty and boys tend not to like me.
- I am terrible at drawing.
- I am bad at expressing my emotions.

THE MOTIVATIONAL PRINCIPLE

Only by shifting our stance from 'I can't' to 'I can', will we be in the running for a better, more fulfilling life that represents who we are today and what we want our tomorrows filled with.

Remember: the excuses we use to avoid doing great things with our lives are a good way of avoiding failure. For example, saying 'I can't lose weight' over and over again to ourselves is a convenient way of continuing to eat all the stuff that is calorific.

When one of these self-limiting beliefs come up, ask yourself:

- Is this really true?
- What am I avoiding?
- What if I changed this belief to 'I can … I will'?
- How would I benefit?

Early recollection – you will paint what we want you to paint

I remember as a tiny child of 3.5 years old being asked to paint a picture. It was a bit like a show and tell art class where the little nursery children would paint something that they had done at the weekend.

I remember standing in front of my easel, all pinnied up, and looking at this lovely white crisp sheet of paper. In front of me were several pots of gooey paint and some brushes stuffed in a jam jar. The classroom smelt of warm milk (in those days we used to have milk delivered every day to the nursery).

While I was getting into my creative process, my mind was cast back to the sunny weekend when we had spent most of our time playing outdoors. It will come as no surprise to you then that I painted a beautiful orange and yellow sun. I was so caught up in the moment and my delicious experience of the colour and heat that the whole canvas ended in a thick layer of yellow-orange paint. Standing up and putting my brush down as if to declare the masterpiece was complete was my first childish error. The teacher approached with an anticipatory smile on her face. Her reprimand was that in my obvious playing around, I had wasted the paint and the sheet. Her words cut through me and etched a deep scar of shame upon my heart. Grabbing my beautiful painting from the table, she unceremoniously tore it up and threw it in the bin. My heart broke into tiny fragments as I wondered what my punishment for being creative and thinking outside the box would be.

Her expectations were of the traditional pretty picture – sky, the sun, flowers, house and a happy family – and I had dared to give her 'abstract expressionism'. Her message was 'expressing yourself gets you into trouble, be what they want you to be'. Imagine a lifetime of such experiences where we see ourselves through the eyes of our significant adults. We are made to see our limitations reflected in their words, their expressions and their negative feedback. They have forgotten what it was like to be a child. In forgetting this, they contaminate our self-esteem, and we begin to formulate negative beliefs about ourselves.

The highly expressive child over time becomes a confused child layered with beliefs such as:

- I am no good at painting.
- I am no good at (you fill in your blanks).

This negative belief of 'I am no good at painting', for instance, in later life can morph into 'I am not good at anything'! This is dangerous and debilitating. Look around you at your friends and family, I am sure you can hear words like this coming from them too. These are the inherited beliefs and mindsets that we need to rewire into positive beliefs or affirmations, as I shall refer to them.

Imagine rewiring 'I am not good at anything' into 'I am good at anything I choose to focus on'. This is a powerful affirmation that gives you a great foundation from which to live your life. Do you think the latter would be a more helpful belief to adopt when you are embarking on something new?

Changing your mindset questions

Never stop challenging yourself with good questions when presented with a challenging situation; do a quick mind flip and ask some open exploratory questions:

- What do I feel great about right now?
- What are my greatest assets?
- What am I super good at?

 Over to you

Quick mindset journalling

Always keep a journal, notebook or a piece of paper and pen handy. You can always find a quiet moment to write and explore. This is super easy, and you can always tell people you had a creative brainwave or an idea that has to be captured. No prizes for guessing who they will be thinking is a super-smart creative type! If you have the luxury of being alone, try recording yourself asking these questions.

Pick up your journal and jot down the following:

- Earliest recollection of being in trouble (you will usually bring to mind something related to this incident, no matter how off the wall that might seem right now).
- What was the incident?
- How did you feel about yourself before the incident?
- What reality or belief did you come away with?
- Do you still have that belief? If yes ...
- How does it limit you?
- How could you change it so it serves you better?
- What difference could this make in your life?
- What will you do next?

By having a handy journal or smartphone where you can record your automatic negative thoughts, limiting beliefs, truisms and saboteur thinking, you will become aware of these almost imperceptible thought processes in your head. Reading them back later is incredibly powerful.

The reason for noting down these thought processes is so that you will become more conscious of them and therefore more in control of them. As they pop into your head, quickly record them in your journal and then translate them into something more positive. For example, 'I can't do ... ' becomes 'I can do ... ' and 'I will do ... '.

Take an 'I can't' statement and repeat 'I can because' silently to yourself, five times for each statement.

As well as your impromptu journalling, I highly recommend you spend 5 minutes every morning and evening repeating the following mantra:

> 'I am abundant and limitless; the physical universe is ready to deliver the resources, people and conditions I need to make manifest my heart's desire.'

This repetition will help you to begin to imagine the right people, circumstances or resources you might need. Stay open and unattached, allowing the universe to deliver.

Just like anything you want to master, this takes time, motivation and energy. If you have never done yoga, you may find even a basic asana difficult at first. Your mind may be telling you *'this is tough, ouch I am stiff, and my knees hurt'*. However, if you stay with it, by the third or fourth week you will find the asana is becoming easier. Your body has created a new muscle memory; where it was awkward at first, now the postures are becoming automatic and flowing. This is exactly how you are going to start training your thought processes from a default negative position to a positive one.

WHY IT IS IMPORTANT TO ENCOURAGE CHILDREN FROM AN EARLY AGE

As a small child, you did not have the maturity to doubt your parents and carers. They were the ones who gave you protection, shelter and food. They may have also been coming from a positive intention to make you better, stronger, safer and trying to protect you. However, while you can forgive them as they were doing the best they could with the resources they had at the time, this does not mean you have to continue to hold their beliefs as true.

Over to you

Your significant adults list

As you learned through RAT, you are heavily influenced as a child by your significant adults. This is an excellent place to start to trace the roots of your beliefs.

- Go back to your significant adults; list and review them.
- This time, you will be jotting down the negative messages you picked up from them.

Some of these messages were not directed at you, but you may have absorbed them without questioning; for example, 'money does not grow on trees' and 'those who want don't get'!

Adopted beliefs vs what I would love

Create two columns in your journal, on the left write adopted beliefs, and on the right the ones you would love instead.

Start by listing the beliefs you have adopted and still hold as true. The common areas where people I have worked with still tend to hold beliefs are:

- money (money does not grow on trees!)
- relationships
- love
- sex
- beauty
- intelligence
- friendship
- health

- old age
- power, etc.

Next, if you could wave a magic wand, list the beliefs you would love to have about yourself.

Make peace with your thought damners

Here is your chance to make peace with the people who have inadvertently damned you. Do the following exercise and then put all of those negative beliefs in a bin and burn them (remember to keep a copy for a later exercise). They do not belong to you anymore; they do not serve you moving forward with your life. You will be choosing new empowering and motivating beliefs instead.

Turning negative beliefs into positive ones

Now that you have your list of significant adults and have started to make peace with them, there is one more step to take before moving on. Get out your journal and write down the following statement:

The negative beliefs I still hold as true are …

Note down any **feelings** you are having about the above.

Once you have your list of all the negative messages you have taken on board and still hold as true, consider things you want to create in your life.

Things I dearly want to create in my life are …

List the **beliefs** that will most serve you in these endeavours.

Go back and review the list of beliefs you would love to have; what else can you add? Could you, in theory, adopt these beliefs as your own?

Yes or no?
>> If no: what are you avoiding and why?
>> If yes: great, go for it. What actions do you need to take to help you take these on board?

Try this: write up your new positive beliefs and put them where you get to see them, for example on your PC or bathroom mirror. The trick is to brainwash yourself, in the nicest possible way.

'I felt I had to prove I was good enough' – Dale

When I met Dale, I was impressed by her outer confidence. She had an MBA and a series of other high-level qualifications. Indeed, she had just taken an NLP practitioners certificate at the same time as taking her ILM Level 7, Executive Coaching Certificate. She was delighted to be one of only two in her ILM class to complete and, although she was tired from studying, she was on a high as she told me about what was next. Her next was two more masters degrees.

When we started to explore why she felt that she needed more qualifications, it soon became apparent that she had a deep need to always do the hardest challenge to prove that she was good enough to be accepted. On further exploration, and with some guided meditation, we soon discovered a school memory.

Although she passed her 11 plus, she heard her teacher telling her father that his daughter would never go to university. This became a self-fulfilling prophecy, because Dale became disruptive at school and eventually was expelled. After a few years in dead-end jobs, she was desperate to prove herself and went to night school. After a few years in other unfulfilling jobs and now married to a man who told her she wasn't good enough to get a degree, she became more and more unhappy.

After one nasty row too many, she enrolled on an MBA course, therefore bypassing the limiting belief that she would never get a degree. Something changed, and she was determined to do better than the school teacher had declared. Only now she was punishing herself by trying to do far too much.

Let's go back to RAT again (the rational mind is there to keep us safe and surviving, and well within our comfort zone). In Dale's case, RAT went into overdrive, and when she was presented with a risk to her survival, she saw that she needed something more so that she could escape her marriage and believed that an MBA was the answer. Not only that, she was quick to sabotage her freedom by filling her time with endless study.

REVIEWING THE MIND YOU LIVE IN

To be happy and fulfilled, as I mentioned in the earlier chapter about saboteurs, we need to rewire ourselves to think in an optimistic and positive way. It's a powerful and transformative paradigm shift that needs to take place.

Choosing the motivation principle approach means you refuse to indulge in self-defeating beliefs. You learn to move into a new realm where your thoughts are viewed as potential realities. What you think, you manifest. You have to manage your RAT chatter towards only thinking of yourself with regard to your capability and awesomeness. I have a placard in my bathroom sent to me by a friend that says 'Don't forget to be awesome'.

Don't forget to be awesome

Abraham Maslow in his hierarchy of needs model describes self- actualized people as individuals who never think about 'what if it does not work' scenarios, These people never clutter their mind with thoughts of potential failure. Rather they use its power to focus on the right people, circumstances or the synchronistic opportunity that will come to them as a result of their envisioning and contemplating the circumstances they do want to create.

When I am feeling a little insecure about something, I read the placard and it sets me up for the day. It also gives me that little lift to focus on all the great things I have done and people I have helped and in an instant I am rewired for that day. Try it for yourself right now.

Think of all the Paralympic champions. They could never have manifested their vision if they were constantly indulging in thoughts of 'what's not possible'. Let's face it, they have every excuse under the sun not to try. However, success and achievement is never about your circumstances and always about your mindset.

This is why reviewing the mind we live in, literally where we live in our head, is our best first step to transforming those negative thought patterns that are giving us excuses for why life is a certain way.

Where do you live in your head?

> An old Cherokee is teaching his grandson about life, 'a fight is going on inside me,' he said to the boy. 'It's a terrible fight, and it's between two wolves. One is evil- he is anger, sorrow, envy, regret, greed, arrogance, self-pity, guilt, resentment, inferiority, lies, false pride, superiority, and ego.'

> He continued 'The other is good – he is joy, peace, love, hope, serenity, humility, kindness, benevolence, empathy, generosity, truth, compassion, and faith. The same fight is going on inside you – and inside every other person too.'

> The grandson thought about it for a minute and then asked his grandfather, 'Which wolf will win?' The old Cherokee simply replied, 'The one you feed'.

In the privacy of our thoughts and in our heads is the wiring of years of experiences that have shaped our perception of ourselves. From some of our earliest recollections, we can probably pinpoint memories where we have not performed in the way our parents and teachers expected us to.

We learn early on how to survive in a world where vulnerability is seen as weakness, and creativity and free expression is viewed as reckless or anti-establishment.

Sir Ken Robinson, in his famous TED talk 'Schools kill creativity', observes that kids are born with genius levels of divergent thinking, i.e. the ability to think creatively. By the time children are 10 years old, they have practically lost their ability to think in this way. Kids start out in life prepared to have a go at all sorts of things, but by the time they are adults they have been 'educated' out of this more carefree, creative way of thinking. He explains that 'if we are not prepared to be wrong we won't come up with anything original'.

We live in a culture that stigmatizes mistakes. Picasso said, 'All children are born artists, the challenge is to remain an artist as we grow old.'

Perhaps you can remember times where you were told:

- 'No.'
- 'That's not good enough.'
- 'Try harder.'
- 'You are not behaving.'
- 'You are too noisy (messy, naughty).'

Whatever the criticism for our failure to deliver the perfect piece of work, picture, or piece of homework, we register a view of ourselves that has been given to us by someone else.

Channel your energy

Rather than spending copious amounts of energy thinking about what we don't want, wouldn't it be great to channel that same energy (being awesome) and attention into what we do want. It is only when we think and contemplate what we desire that we set in motion billions of energy waves and frequencies that are on a mission to create what we have already envisioned (that's coming next). When we use our mind thoughts in this way, miracles begin to happen for us.

Aristotle said that the very act of reflecting on an idea, any idea, sets the process of creation into action – this is an integral component of living a *motivated* 'wired for satisfaction' life.

What you focus on is what you get and the mindset or lens we look at life through will dictate our outcome. Being conscious of these mindsets loosens their grip on us. Becoming more conscious of what they are and writing them down helps to disassociate them from your best self and begins to lessen their power over you.

DISEMPOWERING MINDSETS

We have already explored some of the roots of your beliefs. Now we are ready to consider how the mindsets we adopt can disempower us. Feeling disempowered will leave you feeling less confident and powerless in situations where you would want to be operating at your highest level and being your best self. Some of these mindsets I am sure you will be able to bring immediately to mind. Get out your journal and:

> List the disempowering mindsets you are currently operating out of.

Consider how these mindsets keep you stuck in your comfort zone. In other words – and this is a very difficult concept – *there is always something in it for ourselves when we repeat limiting patterns, i.e. we are usually avoiding confronting something we are holding as a deeper truth.* Read that statement again. It is important to understand that there is something at the root of your mindset that may not be entirely clear at this moment.

For instance, someone who has been hurt in a love affair may have formulated a belief that 'I am bad at relationships'. Which in turn has its reward: 'If I can convince myself I am bad at relationships, I will push everyone away and never run the risk of getting hurt again. Even though I may find partners, I will always cause a breakdown of some sort before it gets too serious. Why? Because I want to protect myself from being rejected.' There is always a payoff behind our negative beliefs, they keep us stuck and on familiar safe ground.

 Over to you

Tackle your mindsets and avoidances

Time to tackle these mindsets and the reward systems we have set up but may have not been aware of. Create two columns in your journal and list some of your well-entrenched negative beliefs on the left, then dig deep to find what you are avoiding on the right-hand side.

Limiting mindset	What am I avoiding?
E.g. I can't lose weight	being loved because I'm not good enough
I am rubbish at relationships	a meaningful relationship, where no one can hurt me
It's difficult to make friends	rejection

Next, coming from your highest self – from that part of you who can rise above the excuses and operate from a place of wisdom – what advice would you give yourself?

Your key roles

It's interesting, isn't it, that we started out listing our significant adults, and now we as adults have roles to play. We bring with us years of beliefs all coming from a place where we trusted others to help teach us the right way. I wonder how all of this impacts the roles you now play. When did you last consider the roles you play and how you play them or the many masks you wear in life? Start thinking of them now.

 Over to you

The roles you play

This time, create four columns in your journal: roles, beliefs, stuck and emotional charge.

Consider what negative beliefs you have of yourself in each role. Select your priority roles from the list below. Consider which ones you feel stuck in and have the most emotional charge about, then reframe them to be more supportive of you.

Roles	Belief	Reframed thought
Mother	It's my job to feed the family	X
Father		
Wife	It's my job to give the family what they need	I need to nurture myself and the family
Husband		
Son		
Daughter		
Friend		
Brother	I have to look after mum	X
Sister		
Husband		
Housewife		
Your job title		
Student		

Once you have done the above exercise, read out the reframed thought to yourself.

Over to you

Rewiring your limiting mindset for satisfaction and fulfilment

Draw up two columns in your journal. On the left write a negative mindset and on the right a new motivating stance.

On the left-hand side, the current belief, note how you feel about yourself in this role. Are you good at it or poor at it? On the right-hand side, what would be more supportive and empowering for you?

Negative mindset/feelings	New motivating stance/feelings
I am a lousy mother	I love my children unconditionally
I am a selfish sister	I reach out to my siblings
I am a lazy student	I can accomplish anything I want

Take this opportunity to transform these negative mindsets before they become self-fulfilling prophecies.

Next put a star against the ones that are most relevant to you and the ones you most want to change. For each, write a sentence on why you want to change and what this will mean to your life.

Busting the myth

Let's continue to examine some of these negative beliefs, e.g. 'I am unlucky in love'. This is also an emotional barrier. Do you remember the negative emotions described in Chapter 3?

This is an 'I can't, I won't' statement coming from the negative GRIEF emotion, which is a victim stance.

There is a checklist for these negative mindsets. It's called busting the myth of negative mindsets: BTM for short (bust the myth). It is a five-step process you can try. Use these points and processes to help you bust the myths of your negative mindsets.

 Over to you

Five-step BTM

Use the previous exercises to help you to flow through the five-point plan.

Step 1: take a negative belief from your list and ask:

- What emotion are you in, e.g. apathy, grief, fear, anger or pride?
- Where did this myth come from?
- What am I avoiding?
- Can I raise my energy and focus on a motivating thought?

Current disempowering belief	New belief
I am a lousy mother	I'm good enough and love my kids
I am dull and unimaginative	I am a positive energy
I am bad with money	I attract what I need
I can't lose weight	I can accomplish anything
I'm unlucky in love	I love myself and attract love

Step 2: what's the motivating thought?

When you say things aloud it changes their energy. Start at the top of your list and say each item out loud to yourself. Note how that feels and where in your body you may be getting a reaction from.

Step 3: busting the myths from your past

Now is the time to review your past and to determine what you heard as a child from various adults around you. It's never too late to change your thoughts, and although you can't change past events you can change the story you tell yourself about them; make peace with it if you will and transform some of those negative views about yourself into motivational life-affirming ones.

Consider this. When you were born you were perfect, the doctor who pulled you out did not say 'Oh we have a baby here who is unworthy, not good enough, shy and timid, not very bright'! How did we go from being a perfect baby to being a person who feels unworthy, not good enough? We were all born perfect with a positive need to express and receive love and affection.

Ask yourself: 'What makes you think you can go through life not loving yourself and getting the love you deserve and need from others?' Of course, some people feel this more strongly than others; it's all relative.

Step 4: limiting beliefs and where they have come from

Any negative views we have of ourselves are based on learned behaviour and ideas we have picked up from others. If a belief does not support you in your present life, you should let it go or transform it. Let's look at some of your negative beliefs and where they come from.

Go back to your significant adults list and review the things that you were told. Make two columns in your journal: on the left the limiting belief, and on the right where it came from.

Limiting belief	Where did it come from?
I'm not good enough	A disapproving father, who was a perfectionist and always wanted more.
I can't trust anyone	A parent who suffered abuse

Step 5: reflection

Reflect on these and ask what purpose they serve you.

Time to defrag your brain

Having completed all of this work, it is time to delete the thoughts that stop you from being wired for satisfaction once and for all. Just as you can defrag a computer, you can do the same to your brain. Imagine your brain as a desktop page on a PC where you have 10 files labelled:

1. My stressful business
2. Things I can't afford
3. What I will do when I have the money
4. My illnesses
5. My unsatisfying relationship
6. My challenging son/daughter
7. Ageing parents

8. My non-existent sex life
9. De-cluttering my house
10. My weight/alcohol problem

If every time you switched on your PC you saw those files, you would be relentlessly draining your energy.

When we clear our desktop of too many files it begins to work more efficiently. Our heads are a bit like this too: the more we ponder and indulge in excuses and limiting beliefs, the more entrenched they become. They take hold and spread. After a while, we begin to expect failure, uncertainty and disappointment as a natural state of affairs. They become truisms that litter our otherwise positive authentic self.

However, it can be different, and you hold the controls. It's a decision, a flick of the switch to a more positive, optimistic and motivated you, but it takes practice and determination to change habits that have been around for many years. We get used to being right about our lives not working. Let's flip a switch and be right about our lives *working* instead. How would that be?

Whatever we focus on tends to show up in our lives, be it what we want or what we don't want. So if we are always talking about what we don't want in our lives, then we tend to create more of the same.

It's important to spend time planting the seeds that you want to germinate. If those seeds are positive affirmations and positive visualizations of what you want to see manifested in your life, this will pay dividends. Remember: the seeds you sow today you will reap tomorrow.

Key thinking points

- Your parents were doing the best they could at the time, with the resources that they had.
- Your negative thoughts are myths coming from a childlike innocence when you were too young to know any better.
- Whatever I choose to believe becomes true for me.
- You can choose to think different, more motivating, thoughts about yourself.
- If beliefs don't serve you, let them go and replace them with supportive ones.
- Your negative beliefs are outdated software that needs to be upgraded.
- You are the author of your universe; you are here to transcend your early limitations.
- When writing the story of your life, don't let anyone else hold the pen.

Practise this daily mantra

'The universe is eager to deliver everything I have envisioned as possible for myself.'

PART THREE

Motivate Your Life: Design the Life You Want to Live

6

Envisioning

....

'The positive thinker sees the invisible, feels the intangible
and achieves the impossible.'

Anonymous

When you pursue your dreams – guided by the values you hold most dear – miracles can happen.

As you begin this final part of the book, take some time to reflect on how far you have come. Next, open your mind to the infinite possibilities that are coming next. Life is made up of many things and at any one time we must be conscious of both what's absorbing our energy and which areas are not getting any of our time and attention.

In this chapter, I am going to be asking you to expand your view of life to include: the relationship you have with your sense of meaning and purpose, your emotional and physical health, your relationships, your sense of well-being, your recreational and social life and your environment. By focusing your attention on these areas, you become more aware of what's missing.

Envisioning is an active internal process; it is the conscious opening up to dimensions and areas in life you have hitherto not considered. It is also the process of diving deep into yourself for those hidden treasures that surface when we ask ourselves the questions:

- What do I want?
- What lights me up?

- What motivates me?
- What gives me meaning and happiness?
- What fulfils me?

Contemplation is the first act of creation.

Aristotle

Envisioning is the process of opening up to your desires and dreams. Daydreaming is a wonderful experience; you can rehearse the future, explore scenarios and go on incredible adventures. Not only that, but you can also use this technique to envision creative ways to solve problems and reach your goals. However, be aware that it can be quite challenging. When you first begin the envisioning process, you may find yourself getting sidetracked by your limiting beliefs. This is perfectly natural. As we have seen in the earlier chapters on RAT and saboteurs, we know that our internal critic and saboteur thoughts can contaminate the creative process and begin to put limits on our dreams and motivations. It is important that when we look through the telescope into the distance, we keep expanding our view and allowing new possibilities to enter into our consciousness.

Do you remember writing your Christmas or birthday list as a child, when you still believed in magic and fully expected your wishes to come true?

Can you remember sitting and wistfully writing your wish list? I invite you to adopt a similar childlike innocence and connect to your wish list with this process.

In that age of innocence, you believed with all of your heart that Santa would deliver; you believed that anything was possible. You need to go back to that place of innocence. Be willing to suspend your current reality and allow yourself to be surprised. Connect with your heart space, that which defies the fierce logic of the rational mind, and feel your dreams.

Envisioning the life you want to create is an art form (think vision boards and writing about perfect days). Not only that, but it is also a discipline that once mastered can become your pot of gold at the end of the rainbow, insofar as what you wish for can and will manifest if your intention and desire are strong enough.

Have you ever tried to stop thinking with your head and start feeling with your heart? Envisioning is heart space contemplation. Bring to mind something that you want. Put your hand on your heart for a moment and take your focus to that space, and consider how differently it feels to want from your heart rather than your head.

MOVING FROM HEAD TO HEART

The journey from the head to the heart is the longest journey you will ever make.

In this chapter, I will be encouraging you to move from the head space, where you have rational, problem solving thoughts, to a heart space, where you can access your spiritual connection about the infinite opportunities that are available to you. The law of attraction (which you will probably have heard lots about already) works on the basis that we attract people who are likeminded. This in itself generates a positive vibe.

The technique of using your imagination (envisioning) to create what you yearn for is a discipline that requires practice to master. This is where you need to be mindful of how you create habits in your life. Creating habits is as unique as you are. Identify a way to make this process a part of your natural waking day and you will have a habit that will serve you forever. Once you have tried this a few times and reaped the benefits, you will be eager to keep practising it.

Visualizing what you want is the ability to use the power of your imagination coupled with a true heartfelt longing for something to manifest. To do this, you must create a mental picture, in whatever way works for you (you can see, sense or think it into place), and increase its intensity by adding in other senses, like a feeling, smell, taste or a sound. As you continue to think about it, build your desire and want it and, finally, expect it. Then continue to focus on the idea, feeling or picture regularly giving it positive vibrations and attention until it manifests in your life.

The realization of what fulfils me changed my life

I used to work in a management consulting practice where I had a great job running large Culture Change and Transformation programs. Life was frenetic, busy and stressful, but we were young and seemed to thrive on it. We worked hard and played hard. Life was an endless procession of exciting projects and parties.

Once I married, I realized that I had been having so much fun I had not paid much attention to having babies. I had put this part of my life on hold. However, time was marching on, and my biological clock was ticking very loudly. Sadly, during this time I lost my beloved mother. This left me emotionally vulnerable and deeply sad. As luck would have it, only a month after my mother's death I found out I was pregnant. However, that ended in a painful miscarriage. This was the last straw; I was emotionally bereft and had hit rock bottom.

I knew I needed to retreat into myself and give myself time to grieve and heal. These events conspired to have me take a long sabbatical from corporate life. It was then I decided I wanted to move out of London and find a peaceful and tranquil environment that was more conducive to creating a family.

Creating my family was not a straightforward path, and my husband Tim and I hit many barriers along the way.

Around this time, my dear friend Anandi – who is a yoga teacher living in Italy – was organizing a yoga retreat for a small group of women. She invited me to run some sessions. After some soul-searching I agreed, this would be the first time in over five years I would be in front of a group, and it filled me with trepidation. In spite of my fears, the retreat went very well and exceeded my expectations on all levels. I was inspired by how rewarding I found this work and thrilled that I was able to make a contribution to these women. It was time to wrap up the retreat, and I decided to run the final Envisioning Process session. Here the group was invited to speed write, beginning their sentences with 'I am fulfilled because … '. The group was instructed to write in the present tense as if it had already happened, and to go into their wish list of everything they wanted to manifest in their lives.

As I sat there in the sunshine surveying the beautiful view and smelling the roses that were in abundance on the terrace of Santa di Stephano in Le Marche, I decided I would start writing too. Then I could gauge how long I should give the group for this exercise. As I wrote, I noticed after about 3 minutes all sorts of interesting hidden treasures surfacing from deep

within me. Deep aspirations that I had never consciously artic-
ulated before. However, there in the lovely sunshine, I found
myself writing:

> 'I am fulfilled because I have two lovely children who are
> happy and healthy running around on the beach ... '

> 'I am fulfilled because I run an International Retreats busi-
> ness for high-level business owners which take place in
> beautiful and exotic places all over the world.'

That was it, I had planted the seeds and envisioned my dream
job and family unit. Aristotle said 'Contemplation is the highest form of activity'. In other words, the challenge for most
people is articulating their heart's desire; once this has been
done activating it is so much easier.

If you cannot imagine what you want, how can you go about
manifesting it?

Within a year of writing that statement all sorts of interesting
serendipitous circumstances presented themselves, which led
me to create the business I own today. Against difficult odds
I have two wonderful children who I adore and who give my
life meaning and purpose.

So be careful what you wish for!

DETOX YOUR HABITS

So many people I meet are not living life to the full; they are
more preoccupied with avoiding failure. How would your life
shift if instead of avoiding failure you targeted success?

To make that shift, before you begin the envisioning process, it is important that you have detoxed some of your negative, habitual, limiting beliefs. Having a positive mental attitude is vitally important because you get in life what you expect; so if you expect positive things to happen, they usually do.

The positive visualizations you conjure up during the envisioning process work are significant (assuming you are disciplined enough to shut off the voices in your head that are arguing for your limitations). Only through doing this can you give your imagination a chance to express itself fully, unencumbered by your limiting beliefs. When successful, this envisioning can transport you to a new realm where you can access a refreshing sense of awareness and where there is peace, possibility and abundance.

 Over to you

Find out what you need to detox

Consider for a moment what makes your feel tired and lethargic. Get out a pen and paper and ask:

- What keeps you feeling stuck?
- How do you know that you are stuck?
- How often do you feel frustrated when you ... ?
- What are your recurring self-limiting beliefs (be honest)?
- What has to happen to make a shift and detox these habits?

As you consider your answers, remember that creating a vision is powerful, and you are only limited by what you consider to be something that holds you back. When you see, feel, hear and have a sense of what you want, this will help to drive your behaviours and actions.

Remembering how to manifest

We all have the power, not just some of us; every human being has the power to manifest great things in their life. The only thing that is stopping you is your willingness to believe in it and imagine yourself with it. It is important that if you say you want a certain job or career, you see yourself with that job and imagine what it will be like to get it.

 Over to you

What do you want?

Try this process:
- Remember a time when you wanted something.
- How old were you?
- What did you want?
- What reasons did you give yourself why you could not have it?
- What did you do to get it?
- How did you feel when you achieved this?
- Bring to mind this time, when you felt successful, resourceful, capable and happy.
- Next, go back to this time of innocence when you believed anything was possible ...

To make this exercise work you have to become you as a child again, full of wonderment, possibility and the certain knowledge that everything and anything was possible.

Put pen to paper and begin to write, or record with no limitations, 'What I want is ... '

For example, as a child I can remember believing that if I walked far enough into the distant horizon, I could touch the sky. What did you believe?

Have you ever wanted something in your life badly, and in spite of difficulties you managed to get that long-desired bicycle, or doll or boyfriend or house?

WHY IT IS IMPORTANT TO VISUALIZE

Science and envisioning

Envisioning, as I have said, is an art form in terms of being a creative process, and life is creation. The scientists who have studied it can additionally offer your rational mind another explanation. Metaphysically speaking, everything is made of matter and energy; matter is stuff that has energy. Things (matter) in our universe that we perceive as separate solid objects – like rocks, mountains, trees, or the ocean – once pared down are all atoms (the smallest pieces of matter). Every atom has electrons (subatomic particles containing an electrical charge), which orbit around the atom's nucleus. Humans are made of the same stuff (matter), albeit arranged in a different way. All of which means that we are all part of one huge energy field. Everything is therefore connected on a metaphysical level. This becomes relevant when we are talking about envisioning and focusing our power to manifest what we want in our world.

Different matter vibrates energetically at different frequencies, and so if you put out positive energy you tend to attract positive energy. This is because you attract towards you matter or people who are vibrating with similar energy. Energy of a certain quality or vibration tends to attract energy of a similar quality and vibration.

You are a part of this magical universal energy, and if you get behind it and harness its power – the power of everything – your life will change.

The vibe of thoughts and beliefs

Even thoughts and beliefs have a positive or negative energy vibe. Have you ever noticed how sometimes you will be thinking about someone you have not thought about for ages, and suddenly they call you? When you put out positive energy and thoughts, you are more likely to attract the same back.

Maybe you have bought or are planning to buy a new car. It is as if there is nothing but this make and model everywhere. All that has happened is that you have become super-conscious of this type of car. There are no more Audis on the road, but you have created a positive awareness around this model of car, and therefore you see it everywhere. You attract towards you what you channel your conscious energy into.

Conversely, if all you think about is the bad things that might happen – for example, how bad people are, how you do not trust anyone or anything and how life always let you down – then guess what? You will probably prove yourself right. After all, as I explained in Chapter 3 *We all have a RAT* (RAT wants to be right), whatever you put much attention and energy into, including your thoughts, is more likely to manifest.

When you are full of fear and insecurity and dwelling on all the bad things that might happen in life, you are more likely to create those negative events.

> **'We are finally living in the house of our dreams' – Sebastian and Willow**
>
> A couple of friends of mine, Sebastian and Willow, had hit a difficult patch in their life; their credit card bills were spiralling

out of control. They felt they had outgrown their existing little house and were yearning to be in a grander home with grounds, a big garden with room for an artist studio (Willow was a professional portrait artist). They had always wanted a dog for their little girls but did not have the space where they were living.

Sadly they had overspent on luxuries and were now feeling overwhelmed and drowning in credit card bills.

During a series of coaching sessions, I suggested that we do the envisioning process and helped them become conscious of a number of their limiting beliefs. These were mainly around money, what they felt they deserved and, more importantly, what they experienced as just out of their reach.

They were now very mindful of the rewiring they had to do. They recited their mantra every morning: 'The universe is waiting to deliver to us the house of our dreams.' They made vision boards of the life they wanted to create and kept looking at their images of their beautiful house, golden Labrador and fine art studio in the grounds.

Six months later the very house they described in their vision boards came up for rent; it had cottages and room for a studio.

Now that they had rewired their thinking and were open to new visions they were able to see the opportunity that presented itself to them. While originally they thought they would have to sell their existing house and save to buy a bigger house, they were now able to see that they could rent their dream house and rent out their own house. At the same time, they were able to turn one of the outbuildings into a wonderful artist studio where Willow could paint, and Sebastian, who was also very creative, repurposed the cottages into upmarket

4-star holiday lets. They now enjoy a lucrative business which is literally on their doorstep. Oh, and yes, they have Oscar their golden lab who the girls adore.

Does this story resonate with you? Do you yearn for your life to be different but experience things being just outside your reach?

 Over to you

Practical visualization and meditations

My next house envisioning

Find a space where you will not be interrupted. Begin to breathe a little more deeply, relax your head and shoulders and gradually slip into a daydreaming space. Let's assume you want to be in a bigger, more beautiful, environment. Begin to imagine what kind of house you will be living in, see yourself walking through the door, perhaps preparing for a dinner party in your beautiful new kitchen. Greeting people as they arrive to celebrate your new found home. Imagine yourself walking them around your beautiful garden and giving them a tour. Feel the feelings of joy and accomplishment, see the smiling faces around you, smell the flowers in the garden, and really make these imaginings come alive.

Then, of course, you have to be willing to take the steps involved in achieving it. This is when magic can happen.

Now have your own visualization, keep creating the picture in every detail. Do this for as long as you need in order to get a detailed image of the thing you want to create.

Write down what comes up for you; go for a walk and reflect. When you come back, we will envision again in a slightly different way.

Envisioning meditation

What do you want?

Get comfortable in your chair or on the floor, close your eyes and notice your breath. Take three deep breaths making sure you are breathing deeply into your stomach. As you gaze into the horizon of your life, begin to bring into view your yearnings, desires and dreams for your future. Your wish list: this is a heart-based contemplation, a quest, a journey of personal discovery. I encourage you to go on an inward journey, imagine yourself devoid of any limitations, excuses or reasons for why you can't have something, be someone who creates something.

As you breathe in, imagine a limitless world where you are free to choose your life.

Let any tension in your shoulders go as you enter your semi-dreamlike space of envisioning the life you will be leading.

What would you be like if you were fully expressed and showing up as the real authentic you in all of your relationships? Being true to yourself and your values. Meandering down the river until you arrive at things, experiences, careers relationships, environments, health, money literally anything that lights you up.

Include areas in life that ordinarily you might overlook or forget to focus on unless you were encouraged.

When you have finished, grab your journal. Ask yourself the qualifying questions:

- Do I really want it?
- Am I prepared to do what it takes to have it?
- Am I prepared to take the consequences of having x manifest in my life?

If the answer to all these questions is a resounding 'yes', then you should go for it!

Once again, go for a walk and reflect. On your return make a note of what comes up for you.

Bonus meditation

A 10-minute meditation is available on my website if you wish to use it at this stage.

Now that you have become aware that your thoughts can be managed and trained to contemplate the more positive, you are ready for the next exercise.

 Over to you

'I am fulfilled because … '

Sit down somewhere comfortable, perhaps overlooking a lovely view, where you won't be interrupted. Make sure you are breathing into the whole body, especially the abdomen. As you breathe deeply and imagine that you are one lung with the universe, begin to let your consciousness rise up into your third eye (located between your eyes).

Project into your best future and begin to imagine everything that could possibly fulfil you. As little saboteur thoughts try to pop up, like *'that's a bit much!'*, let them float away. In a moment, you are going to begin to craft your future. Imagine that everything you write is the act of planting the first little seedling. Your only limitation is your own imagination. When you are ready to put pen to paper, begin to write in your journal:

> I am fulfilled because …

Write in the present tense as if everything you want has already happened. Except this is 2–10 years from now depending on how far out you want to envision.

> I am fulfilled because …

Keep writing until you have filled several pages. At first, it may feel difficult to come up with the envisionings, but as you write you will release a stream of consciousness that might surprise you. This is a bit like a brainstorm (there is no such thing as a bad idea).

I have worked with literally hundreds of people and, believe me, this works!

You must approach this exercise with the following in mind:

- Like a brainstorm, there is no such thing as a bad idea.
- No holds barred.
- Unplug your cynical, negative voices that are arguing for your limitations.
- Keep writing until your pen takes on a mind and energy of its own.

- Give it at least 15 minutes; it will be slow at first as you get the wheels oiled but within 5 minutes or so you should be on a roll.
- Now read back what you have written.
- Note down in your journal:

How will I feel if all this comes about?

When do I want this to come about?

What year will it be? e.g. 2017.

What age will I be?

FINDING YOUR LEARNING STYLE

Everyone has an optimum way of processing information. Your learning style is a combination of how you perceive, then organize and process, information. When you are familiar with your preferred learning style, you can take important steps to help yourself to envision more easily.

It is important that you try different methods to access what's important to you and what you want to envision for your future. NLP, or neurolinguistic programming, holds that every individual has three channels for receiving information. These channels are: visual – through pictures; kinesthetic – through feelings; and auditory – through sounds.

Visual – some people will respond to the visual imagery they see.
Kinesthetic – some people will feel emotional about the experiences they want.
Auditory – some people will respond better to sounds.

Make sure you try different methods and see, feel or hear which system is your preferred modality.

For the visuals

Creating your vision board

A vision board is a collage filled with images, words and statements that reflect the desire and energy you want to manifest in your life. When you use a vision board, you are simply creating something tangible that reinforces the positive thoughts in your mind and invites more of that energy into your environment. When you place it somewhere you can see, every day you are visualizing your creation into reality.

Find somewhere you can spread out on to, a big table or floor.

You will need:

- A few large blank quality sheets of heavy paper.
- Magazines.
- Images/photographs.
- Snippets/headlines (choose pictures that resonate with what you want).
- Glue and scissors.

Begin to imagine all the experiences and things you want in your life. Visualize what your life would look like in the future and consider: What do you yearn for?

- A beautiful house perhaps, lovely children, a loving relationship, more money, a fit body, regular yoga practice.
- A house in the sun overlooking a coast.
- Signing books as you have just written your bestseller, running your new business.

Begin to collate them on to your large sheet, laying them in a way that feels right; give them a sense of place.

Once you have finished, stand back and look at your life. There may be other finishing touches you want to include.

Once you are happy with your creation, place it in a prominent position where you can see it every day when you wake up.

Remember: each time you look at your vision board and reflect, you are creating new neural pathways. This neural network will help you to notice more opportunities day to day that will help you to achieve your vision. Feel free to add images that you come across.

For the auditory people

In addition to creating a vision board and in a similar way, you can begin to collate an auditory board. Collect together sounds that have resonance for you. Arrange them in a folder with names that mean something. For example, you could create a guided meditation or a playlist of songs. Play the songs when you want to envision the future. Anchor sounds and desires.

For the kinesthetics

People who are kinesthetic need to feel an experience. A vision board can be used as it will conjure up all kind of emotions as you look at it. However, you may also want to create a vision board that is more tactile. Think about how things feel to the touch as well as when you look at them. You could, for example, make your collage out of books, fabric and materials that hold an emotional expression for you. However you have created your vision board, remember to look at it afterwards and take time to reflect and keep asking the physical universe for what you want. The bigger the desire, the bigger the delivery from the universe.

To allow yourself to dream, imagine and desire new experiences – such as great relationships, optimum health and fitness, a dream job/career, a baby, a new home, whatever it may be – you have to believe that you can make it happen. Envisioning and fully intending for it to come about plants the seeds out there and the universe will undoubtedly deliver. Stay with it and don't give up at the first hurdle!

Key thinking points

- You can create the life you desire by focusing on what you wish to attract.
- Spend your energy well by contemplating what it is you want to manifest in your life and imagine yourself having the life you have created in your mind's eye.
- The universe will begin to create circumstances, opportunities and resources that you will now notice and take advantage of.
- Focus on what you want, not what you do not want.
- You get in life what you focus on, so if you focus on the difficulties and challenges these will show up and take centre stage.
- Surround yourself with positive people who back your vision and believe in you.

Practise this daily mantra

'I create my own reality and choose abundance and possibility.'

7

Life Planning –
The Day to Day

'To reach a port we must sail, sometimes with the wind, and sometimes against it. But we must not drift or lie at anchor.'

Oliver Wendell Holmes

Turning visions into reality is when alchemy occurs.

Now that you have envisioned what you want to create in your life, the next step is to make sure you have a practical plan to achieve it. Sounds easy; however, having a plan is one thing, and making it happen is another. In this chapter, I will be sharing with you a life planning method that I and many of my clients have utilized with very successful results. I will also be introducing you to selection criteria that will assist you in prioritizing so that the right things are getting your attention and energy.

This book started with you exploring what some of your dearest values are and the kind of qualities you want to have centre stage in your life, e.g. love, health, happiness and contribution.

During one of your visualizations, you may have envisioned yourself as a healthy older person, with masses of energy and vitality: e.g. when I am 60 years old I want to be healthy, active, ski and still be a healthy weight. It is important to work backward from this visualization to the practical implications for today. I have a little rule which is: 'what gets scheduled gets done'.

If you schedule in your diary three activity sessions, i.e. swim, gym, walk, tennis or run, you are setting up the conditions for success. Remember what I said about routines and rituals when we discussed purpose? These activities have to be scheduled into the fabric of your week, or they won't get done. If you want to have health and vitality in your 60s, 70s and 80s you have to begin to create rituals and good habits today that will naturally lead you there.

CREATING YOUR LIFE-ENVISIONING PLAN

A life-envisioning plan takes into account every aspect of your life. Most people understand the concept of project planning. If you want to build a house you may have a visual idea of what you want to build, architectural plans and then a meticulous step-by-step process that once followed will achieve the result.

Even though this house may take a year or two to build, you know that you have to take practical steps today to have it come about. For example, the first thing you might do is call an architect and commission him to create the drawings.

Life-envisioning planning is similar except that, rather than planning one project at a time, there will be a number of areas you will be focusing on. As the diagram shows, we always begin with what is driving you from your core. You begin at your core values, which we discovered in Chapter 1. These will always be your compass that will help you get back onto your path should you lose your way in the busyness of life.

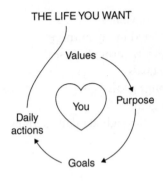

THE LIFE YOU WANT

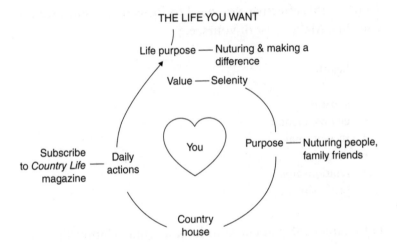

THE LIFE YOU WANT

Values-based life-envisioning planning model

The values-based life-envisioning planning model takes you through a process that sees you taking daily action to reach your goals through the values you decide to life your life by. You are now on a journey from values to leading a truly purposeful life. The steps in the process are:

1. living by my core values
2. which are reflected in my purpose
3. created specifically through these
   a. long-range goals
   b. medium-range goals
   c. short-term goals
4. and carried out through my daily actions.

Key life areas

To make this effective, you need to focus on the key areas of your life. Make a list of yours, e.g:

- health
- family
- spiritual
- environmental
- recreational
- financial
- relationships
- professional.

For example, if you chose to look at your relationships, ask yourself:

- How do my core values affect how I conduct my important relationships?
- How are these reflected in my purpose?
- What are my long-, medium- and short-term goals around relationships?
- What daily actions do I need to take to ensure I meet these goals and am living a purposeful life according to my core values?

Over to you

Planning the life you want

To start this process, go back to your visualization and vision board and remind yourself of what you see as your future. Use the life planning worksheet, which is available to download from my website.

Life-envisioning master matrix

1. Across the top, specify the key areas of your life (e.g. business, career, relationships, family, personal development).
2. Where you see values along the side, write in your top five to eight values.
3. Next, write in your purpose.
4. Select an area of your life.
5. Choose a value and create your value statement where the area and the value intersect.
6. Specify your ten-year goal, five-year goal and one-year goal for this area.
7. Review your matrix and put it somewhere you can see as you will be referring to it daily.
8. Do this for all of your areas, or at least as many as you can that make sense to you. You may want to do this in several sittings.

Your daily actions

Use the daily planner I have provided for the next stage; when you are doing this on a regular basis, you may want to switch to an electronic calendar or use your desk diary.

What are the daily actions you need to take to reach each of your goals?

Life envisioning master matrix

Values	Values statement	Business (1)	Learning (2)	Relationships (3)	Financial (4)	Well being (5)	Creative (6)	Spiritual (7)	Community (8)	Travel (9)	Me time (10)	AN Other (11)
1												
2												
3												
4												
5												
6												
7												
8												
9												
10												
11												
12												
13												
14												
15												
16												
17												
18												
19												
20												

Purpose

Goals

Long term

1

2

3

Medium term

1

2

3

Short term

1

2

3

Daily planner

Daily values based actions											
RASOR your actions											
Values	Business (1)	Learning (2)	Relationships (3)	Financial (4)	Well being (5)	Creative (6)	Spiritual (7)	Community (8)	Travel (9)	Me time (10)	AN Other (11)
1											
2											
3											
4											
5											
6											
7											
8											
9											
10											
11											
12											
13											
14											
15											
16											
17											
18											
19											

Vital versus urgent

Now that you have begun to build your life plan, the next step is to look at 'vital versus urgent'. This is where you prioritize the most relevant actions over the seemingly important. Once you have a broad idea of your life plan, you must be able to apply the very important criteria of distinguishing the vital actions over the urgent actions.

- VITAL means life force, life enhancing, irreplaceable.
- URGENT means demanding your immediate attention (usually someone else's priority).

Review your vital vs urgent

Have a go at marking up your daily activities as either vital or urgent. We will be applying a process to them later. For now, I want you to try and determine as best you can what they are.

BEING IN OVERWHELM

I have coached people who are in so much overwhelm with so many seemingly urgent things to do that they literally can't see the wood for the trees. They talk about work life balance, but they are totally out of balance. They have hundreds of demands on them coming from so many different directions that they have lost their ability to choose where to put their energy. They are drowning in a world of top priorities and information overflow. They are asking themselves: What should I be reading? Should I be on LinkedIn? I really need to see my Mum or Dad this weekend, but how can I fit them in? What TED talks do I make time to listen to? What should I be subscribing to; I don't want to miss anything?

This sort of thinking results in umpteen e-mails that they have to spend an hour a day or more deleting because they have lost their ability to filter the vital from the urgent. Learning to filter, prioritize, say NO to other people's demands becomes critical to their own sense of satisfaction and fulfilment. Becoming crystal clear about what is vital in your life – e.g. life enhancing and activating core values, versus urgent – demanding your immediate attention, is essential to the successful implementation of your plan.

Life presents us with wonderful opportunities every day – if we have not clarified what's important to us in our hearts, and understand at a deeper level why we need to be here rather than there, we will be missing the opportunities that life is offering us every day to be great, happy, fulfilled and satisfied.

In the absence of the ability and personal discipline to distinguish the vital actions and demands from the seemingly very important, we deprive ourselves of a very special gift: space. Yes, space to figure out what's good for us, what makes our energy soar, what nourishes us on a deeper and enduring level. We have no space to be satisfied because we are too busy chasing our tails. Like the proverbial rat in the rat race, the faster the rat runs, the faster the wheel goes. Have you ever felt your life is running away with you? When do you get off the wheel and decompress, take stock, allow the busyness of your life to subside, so that you can recreate order and then some SPACE? Space in your head, to have a longer view and perspective about your life. If you are busy drowning in trivial/urgent actions you never give yourself the space and time to consider what's vital and life enhancing.

It's probably safe to assume that, like me, you have a full and busy life. For me, that means one minute I am jetting off to run an intensive three- or four-day retreat, and the next I am back at home fully in demand as a mum, wife, friend, coach. Yes, I have a lot to juggle, and I have to make some ruthless and radical choices if the important things in my life are going to continue to bring me satisfaction and meaning. I owe it to my family and clients that I don't become burnt out, as nobody will win in that scenario.

Sometimes when I feel I am going slightly out of kilter – i.e. I am overscheduled and have not left enough of a buffer for my exercise, sleep, me time – I immediately get a big alarm going off in my head, and I know it is time to put on the brakes, edit, simplify and re- prioritize. This may mean turning work away, literally deleting certain meetings, get togethers and casual phone calls that are cluttering up my days. I still have a desk diary, because in some ways I am still a bit of a dinosaur and enjoy the touchy feely sensation of having a real solid book to write in.

When I have reached these moments of sheer overwhelm I take out my eraser and begin to rub out the clutter in my desk diary. I make a note of what needs to be cancelled or moved. I apply certain criteria such as: Will this action contribute to my longer-term purpose and direction? Will seeing this person, doing this action bring me any closer to fulfilling my vital goals? Ultimately, I am asking *is this in line with my purpose*? If the answer is NO, then when I am in overwhelm I begin the business of 'pruning' – cutting out the dead wood, if you will, to let the delicate buds flower. This is a bit like gardening. Those of you who have green fingers, have you ever considered what would happen to your garden if you never got rid of the weeds or if you or your gardener never pruned the rose bushes, never cut out the woody stalks of your lavenders? Well if you did not do any of these actions regularly and seasonally you would be looking at an overgrown untidy garden but, worst of all – and this is where this metaphor takes on a more sinister significance for your life – sooner or later the weeds would strangle the beautiful roses. **The roses are your dreams – your vital goals – give them a chance to flower and blossom.**

Cultivating a beautiful garden takes commitment, dedication and regular seasonal activities. If you do not plant the bulbs in winter, you cannot look forward to the magnificence of spring flowers shooting out of the ground and casting their fragrance in the air. It's at this stage in the year we either celebrate our forward thinking and our diligent winter planting or regret having missed the boat! Remember: you reap what you sow and **if you are not planting your dreams in fertile soil, they will not come to fruition.**

Creating space for self-nurturing, decompressing and rebooting is essential to my well-being. If you do not take the time out you will soon be running on empty.

When you begin to approach overload you probably notice these typical signs:

1. You feel de-motivated, fed up, and become irritable and grumpy.
2. Your energy goes down when you look at your gruelling schedule.
3. You begin to future your life to the oasis of free time you can see down the line.
4. You stop being present and begin to go into automatic pilot mode.

5. The meaning that you normally experience in your day-to-day work is replaced by a feeling of hard slog, and a yearning for the end of the day to come when you can rest.

Does this sound familiar? If the answer is YES, then this is when it's essential to **STOP and begin to cut out the clutter.**

RASOR your actions

RASOR stands for review, audit, simplify or reprioritize:

- Review your daily actions.
- Audit by asking: Are they vital or urgent?
- Simplify by cutting out any dead wood, being ruthless (using your qualifying questions) and making radical and unreasonable decisions, clearing space and opening up opportunities.
- Or Reprioritize as appropriate (using your qualifying questions).

'I finally stopped prioritizing my urgent over my vital needs' – Natalie

A couple of years ago I was facilitating a retreat, and a lady walked in who I shall call Natalie. She was very beautiful but was obviously struggling with her weight. During her disclosures, she let us know that she was totally exhausted and stressed out.

During our discussion about what she was prioritizing in life, she came to the realization that she had been so busy climbing up the corporate ladder that she had put her private life on hold. As a result, she was struggling to have a baby so now was on her third round of IVF. Because of the stress she had gained 5 stone and she spent the whole workshop in floods of tears realizing that she had cheated herself out of the life she deserved.

A year later when I saw her again, she was completely transformed. After having applied the vital versus urgent criteria, she made some radical, unreasonable decisions.

She had left her job and had taken a well-deserved sabbatical; she had adopted a ruthless dieting regime, which meant she had lost 4 stone; and she was well on her way to creating a new, happy, and more fulfilled life with her new fiancé.

Sadly her IVF was unsuccessful, but at least she was able to be a mother to her fiancé's children. Natalie had made a decision to be FREE. She had finally stopped prioritizing her urgent over her vital needs.

Creating the space for the life you want to manifest

Have you ever noticed how liberating it is to have a clear out at home – that old cupboard, shelf, spare room, wardrobe. It is sometimes an uncomfortable process, and some people are real hoarders as they are so attached emotionally to their objects, clothes and photographs.

However, if we never throw stuff out, we would literally get trapped in our overcrowded and overcluttered rooms. I am sure we all know a hoarder who lives in the midst of their clutter. This is not a healthy way to live, and often these hoarders eventually seek professional help to assist them to make the ruthless decision to get rid of stuff so they can physically enter their own rooms.

I remember a documentary about one poor hoarder who could not see her floor anymore. She had to live in a tiny space with no room to actually lie properly on her bed as it was covered with clothes and magazines and stuff she could not bring herself to throw out.

She had lost friendships and had alienated her family, as she was so scared of their judgements and feedback, and no one was allowed over her threshold. She had prioritized her clutter over her relationships and ultimately the quality of life.

Now I know I am talking about extremes here; however, when was the last time you had a good spring clean of your life?

When I was a sales executive and was eager to get my quota for the month – which would mean lots of validation, commission and, quite frankly, an easy life – I would do anything to ensure I was on target at the end of every month.

When I felt I had done everything in my power to get my orders in for that day, and I literally could do nothing else, I began to clean my space, throw things away to freshen up my office and basically handle any outstanding tasks and bills (clutter); and sure enough when everything was in order and in its place the phone would start ringing, fax machines would start rattling with orders trying to get through. I can't explain these phenomena, but in my case and many of my colleagues' cases it seemed to work.

When we create space in our lives, we make way for new opportunities to come in.

Over to you

Implementing the RASOR criteria on your working week

Start this process with your life-envisioning master matrix in front of you.

- Start with your values as an organizing principle and ask: Which value am I honouring today?
- Have your weekly planner in front of you.
- Add in your daily actions, if you haven't already done so.
- Apply RASOR.

Review and audit

Look at your list of activities for this week and ask:

- Is this activity in line with my purpose and values?
- Will doing this activate one of my highest values?
- Will this activity allow me to be my best self?
- Is this an appropriate way to use my time?
- Will this action give me a massive and enduring payoff?
- Does my energy soar at the prospect?

QUALIFYING QUESTION

Apply your qualifying question to each action.

- Is this activity vital or urgent?

Remember: feeding yourself a diet of vital activities will have a massive and enduring payoff.

IMPORTANT: Looking at your working week, make sure you have sprinkled a number of vital activities in your daily planner. For example, let's say that one of your top values that you want to be activated more fully in your life is friendships. You must ensure that you have scheduled this precious time into your planner, that you have literally diarized your vitals as well as your must dos and urgents.

Simplify or reprioritize

Look at your map of your week and see what you can simplify or cut out to create the space for your vitals.

EXAMPLE OF A DAILY/WEEKLY PLANNER

MONDAY
    Call to make an arrangement with a friend/friends
TUESDAY
    Go for a run
WEDNESDAY
    Go to yoga
THURSDAY
    Take the children to the cinema
FRIDAY
    Meet friends for drinks

If meetings come up, prioritize your vitals over your urgents and very rapidly you will see your life take a different direction. Your life will take a direction toward more satisfaction and fulfilment. This activity takes radical unreasonableness, but if you don't apply radical unreasonableness to the way you spend your time, someone else will.

Completing this exercise should help you to realize that skipping going to the gym or having a run may seem fine in the context of the very important meeting that has come up, but this mindset tends to become habitual. If you are willing to do it once or twice, you are creating a subliminal willingness to keep giving in to things that seemingly are more important than your health. **Nothing is more important than your health**. That meeting can be scheduled later in the day or at a time more convenient to you.

We have to consciously create regular good habits. Have you ever tried to lose weight? If you have ever tried and been successful, you will know what I mean when I say the devil is in the detail. It's not the one chocolate or drink or portion of fries that puts on the weight, it's the habitual and repetitive willingness to give into these temptations that lets us down. Once we have made a decision that we are determined to lose weight, nobody can tempt us. It's easy.

Let us take another value I often hear on my retreats and workshops. People tell me family and their kids are their top priority, but on closer examination they are expending a lot of energy feeling guilty about not being available for them. They get home after the kids are asleep, someone else picks them up and drops them off, and they suddenly wake up when their kids are teenagers and wonder when did that happen? This lost time can never be retrieved.

If family/your kids really is a top value, ask yourself:

When was the last time you read your kid/s a bedtime story?
When was the last time you picked them up from school and surprised them with a treat?
Played with them their favourite game?
Found a common language?

Have you been too busy providing to be there?

To summarize, living a life according to your highest values means being able to say NO. This method for being more efficient, productive and effective in both your personal and professional life will highlight for you a way of distinguishing the vital activities, which are few, from the seemingly urgent many. Feeding the vital life-giving activities that nourish your soul, rather than putting copious amounts of energy into the junk that will always be there demanding your immediate attention.

For instance, if you don't switch off your mobile when you are having a romantic dinner with your wife on her birthday, a ringing cell phone can break that moment of intimacy and literally ruin the atmosphere. We are allowing ringing phones to urgently draw us into seemingly important tasks when actually, if it was that important, they could ring back at a more convenient time.

A good example of a vital activity over an urgent one is people's addiction to their mobiles. When I am working with a group, one of my first ground rules for the day is NO phones or other technology in sight. I sometimes have to collect them up, as the addiction to taking a peek is so great. I invite them to go on a cell phone diet for the day (or in severe cases at least until lunchtime) and I can literally see a sea of horrified faces at the prospect of being cut off from their life support machines for any length of time. However, at the end they are fine; no one has died, and everybody is OK.

At least they have been fully present; they have backed their decision that this day is for them and agreed to the conditions that will serve this purpose.

The key message here is that if you want a life that is fulfilling and aligned with your purpose you have to get radically passionate about guarding what you want and getting rid of everything else. It's simple but takes courage, commitment and a willingness to change the habits of a lifetime.

Key thinking points

- Always plan from your core values.
- Keeping the life-envisioning master matrix in sight is similar to keeping your vision board in sight – it is a very powerful reminder.
- As you create daily actions, always make sure you can easily distinguish the vital tasks from the urgents.
- Ensure you have a regular de-weeding process so that you can prioritize the actions and pursuits that will let your dreams germinate and grow.
- Be ruthless and manage the saboteur voices arguing for your limitations.
- Take time out with yourself at least once a quarter to stand back and decompress and reprioritize.

Practise this daily mantra

'I have the life I want.'

8

Taking Care of Your Biggest Asset – You

....

'Your present circumstances don't determine where you can go; they merely determine where you start.'

Nido Qubein

This is it! You have arrived with a fresh mindset and are already working towards creating the life you want. You are now ready to make sure that you continue to look after your biggest asset – you, for the rest of your life.

Throughout these chapters, you have learned how to get in touch with what you want out of life. You have discovered what values you want to activate more fully in your life so that you can create more meaning and purpose. I hope we have also managed to raise your consciousness on how your rational mind can sabotage you and your best-laid plans.

We have explored how habitual limiting beliefs curtail your ongoing development and willingness to take a risk and leave your comfort zone. You have created a vision and a life plan that is motivating and inspiring you. The final step now is to live a congruent life, which reflects the values you hold most dear.

It is vital you take care of your biggest asset.

YOU – YOUR BIGGEST ASSET

In this chapter, I will be sharing with you a holistic review of all the other rituals that could help you to prioritize your fulfilment so that you constantly have renewable sources of energy, e.g. diet, exercise and meditation. It is important to create daily rituals and routines to keep you motivated, on track and in the direction of your highest priorities.

But before we do so, I would like you to do a little review of where you are today with your self-nurturing.

Quiz

Please answer yes or no to the following questions.

Mind

You like/love yourself

1. You prioritize having joy, fun and happiness in your life.
2. You declutter your unhealthy relationships regularly.
3. You have a supportive peer group.
4. You are reading, attending seminars, workshops or retreats for your own personal development.
5. You check e-mails at specific times and avoid looking at them at the weekend.

Body

You are happy with your physical body

1. You eat a healthy, varied diet.
2. You avoid alcohol three days per week.
3. You take some regular exercise, e.g. walk, swim, cycle, yoga, workout.

4. You regularly get 7–8 hours sleep.
5. You go for regular medical check-ups, e.g. women and men's clinics.

Spiritual/emotional

1. You live your values.
2. You do some form of mindfulness or relaxation technique.
3. You keep a journal and have goals and aspirations.
4. You are up to date with your friends and family.
5. You see your kids and spend quality time with them (if relevant).
6. You have a healthy attitude towards money.

How did you do?

If you answered 'No' to more than five of those questions you probably need to channel some more love and attention towards yourself. The rest of this chapter will help you create a checklist of new habits and rituals that will help you feel more motivated, purposeful and fulfilled.

YOU ARE YOUR BIGGEST ASSET

You are the sum of all of your personal experiences, the choices you have made, your stories, the people you have met and the values you live your life by. You can sit passively by, or you can play a larger role in the asset that is you. One of the benefits of not sitting and watching your life pass you by is that by making the choice to change you will undoubtedly be better able to accept changes if they are thrust upon you.

First you need the desire to change. Second, you need to take action. Then you need to review and start again. This audit is something that should be done on a regular basis. Just as the seasons constantly move, so do you.

TAKING CARE OF ALL OF YOU

What I have discovered, as have my clients, is that taking a decision to love and take care of all of you – mind, body and spirit – is the difference that makes the difference. The relationship you have with you is the first thing to address. Once you have made a decision to love yourself and stop abusing your body, whether you are starving it or stuffing it, you will find everything else will fall into place.

Think about it: dieting only seems to work when you invest the time to make a radical change. As soon as you become bored with it, or it appears to no longer work, it seemingly fails. What you need to do is make small, incremental changes in all areas of your life – e.g. routines, exercise, food – because they are all linked. Most importantly, it is how you think about your health that will make the biggest difference.

Let's tackle the physical first. If the human container does not get nourished, then all of the systems that rely on that nourishment will fall over. Just as if you do not look after the hard drive on your computer, one day you will find that there is no longer any room for it to work at its most efficient level.

Mind

Nurture yourself
Part of nurturing ourselves is being loving and approving of us. Rather than listening to the choir of internal critics, let's

try transforming those voices into ones of love and approval. Imagine what your life would be like if every time you looked in the mirror you acknowledged yourself. How many times do we look in the mirror to find the fault, the spot, the blemish? Begin to change the relationship you have with yourself and you will see your life fully reflecting this change.

 Over to you

'I approve of myself because … '

Before you go any further, please take a few moments to do this activity. Grab a pen and your journal and begin to write. Just put your pen to paper and do not think or rationalize. When you first start you may find it stilted, but trust the process and keep going.

I approve of myself because …

When you have finished, ask if there is anymore and then go and grab a cuppa. When you come back, read the list and ask yourself how you feel now that you can see what you approve of.

This is a wonderful exercise. Do it on a regular basis, I recommend at least twice a week as you are going through the *Motivate Yourself* programme. It will, I promise, keep you motivated and on track.

Give to increase joy and happiness

The simplest way that I know to create joy and happiness is to smile every day and use this give process.

Give away: in other words declutter and give away what you no longer need.

Give up: let go of those things that you do not need, processed food, bad habits, toxic friends.

Give in: surrender to what you need to thrive.

Give to others: maybe your time or a listening ear.

Give to yourself: what would make you appreciate you more?

Give thanks: say thank you for your abundance.

Say goodbye to toxic relationships

We live in a society that has hitherto not encouraged people to be open and honest with each other. The stiff upper lip era, where people put up with toxic relationships, is over. We now live in a new time where people are recognizing the damage that is caused by putting up with things and people in our lives that drain our energy and are either consciously or unconsciously upsetting us on a regular basis. There should be a government health warning on these people.

This relationship could damage your health

I wonder which relationships are damaging your health? This could be from personal relationships with our other halves, teenagers, to our bosses, work colleagues and staff. Think for a moment about people who you feel have upset you in the last week. Why was that? Did you misread their intentions? Did you fail to give feedback in the moment that you felt irked by them?

Have you noticed that when you feel someone has upset you in some way, and you let it pass without mentioning anything, the next day they may do something else – and you let this go too as you tell yourself you have a problem with confrontation? Sooner or later you begin to avoid that person and before long you can't even make eye contact. You begin to build a whole reality based on the negative experience. What if you changed your thinking and brought it up with the one person who can make a difference to you?

Take it to the source

Giving people honest feedback in the moment is far healthier than keeping things bottled up. To do this you will need a little courage; make sure that you are assertive and not aggressive in your response. You can be honest in a gentle and diplomatic way. It's always worth talking to the offending person directly rather than going round the houses getting everyone else to agree with you. People will respect you for being honest and speaking your mind.

Watch your peer group

We tend to become like the people we hang around with. When you have taken a decision to make a change in your life, whether it be stopping smoking, losing weight or going on some personal development seminar, the people around you change. Have you noticed how some of your 'friends' can be a little cynical and come out with comments like 'Oh no what training have you been on now?' or 'Can't you stop smoking tomorrow after my party?'

These are unhelpful comments and the last thing you need when you are trying to give up addictions and are struggling with change. What you don't need is people around you not giving you any encouragement and trying to keep you the same or trip you up. The reason being that if they were to fully and genuinely support you in your decision to make a change, they would have to take a big look at their own life. If you are successful at whatever you have chosen to do, you could be invalidating their life choices in some way and high-lighting for them their lack of drive and vision.

Surround yourself with people who are also making those good decisions. For instance, if you want to lose weight, statistics show that people who join a weight watching support group are four times as likely to be successful and stay with the process and lose weight.

If you want to make changes in your life following a personal development seminar, it is better to hang around some of the other attendees who are inspired about making those changes. You have to surround yourself with a like-minded peer group to support and validate the changes you are making.

 Over to you

Get your relationships up to date

- Make a list of your natural universe, i.e. people you come in contact with regularly, work colleagues, staff, neighbours, other parents at the school gate, friends and family.
- Once you have listed their names, write by the side of their name if you feel happy with where you are in the relationship or not.
- Does your energy go up when you think about them? If you see their name on your mobile are you prompted to answer immediately, or do you let it go to voicemail? Are you looking forward to the next time you meet? Or does your energy plummet because you feel that there is some outstanding communication still to be sorted out? Is it a thumb up or down? Maybe you are getting a horizontal thumb, i.e. neither an up nor down, just an OK.

Whatever the energy level, wouldn't it be great if you got a raised energy feeling with everyone in your immediate universe? In other words, you were up to date and feeling positive with everyone. Remember, one of the biggest regrets of the dying is incomplete relationships. They hang out there like an infected limb needing to be healed or severed. If you don't cut off a diseased limb it tends to infect the whole body with gangrene poisoning. Similarly, diseased relationships need to be healed, sorted out, or we have to find a way to forgive and move on if we are going to feel more present, motivated and happy in our lives.

What actions will you take to bring these relationships into balance and harmony?

If you are waiting for an apology or a phone call or you are carrying around some old wound or past hurt, consider forgiving that person and bringing the relationship up to date in any way you know how. Maybe you could make a call, send a card or create a reason to talk to them to clear the air.

This way you stop being a victim of your circumstances and you begin to take responsibility for the outcome you want to have manifest and come about. Stop waiting for other people to make the first move if the relationship is a drain on your energy: sort it out.

Invest in your personal development
Reading this book and taking action is making an investment in your personal development. As is taking the time out for retreats, workshops and personal coaching. You are worth it. Put aside some of your income (profit) to invest in making you the best you possible.

Go on a digital diet
Make a rule not to check work e-mails, your iPhone or watch TV for one day at the weekend.

Pets are good for the soul

Pets provide us with unconditional love and affection. My little cocker spaniel Coco is a bundle of pure love, playfulness and joy. It's a challenge to stay serious for too long when she is around. Our pets help us to express our love on a daily basis, to give strokes and affection. It can become easier to express love to loved ones and humans if we have daily practise with our beloved pets.

Dogs, for instance, are a great way to ensure you are forced to get regular exercise. Cats can help us calm down as we stroke them, and little furry creatures like hamsters are a great way to encourage children to take responsibility for cleaning their cage and making sure they get fresh food.

Body

Detox your thoughts and your lifestyle will follow!

I've noticed that as people start to 'detox' their minds of negative and limiting beliefs, the body usually follows. When we are thinking more positively about who we are and what we can create in life, and when we are fully engaged and motivated, this in turn usually leads to a total overhaul of mind, body, and spirit. As you raise your consciousness in one area of your life, you begin to notice other ways you are sabotaging yourself.

Illness and disease can often be triggered by deep feelings of betrayal, not feeling supported in life, lack of self-worth and a myriad of past hurts and grievances we hold on to. When we are ill at ease, this can cause disease. Well-known author Louise Hay (*You Can Heal Your Life*) talks about how illness and disease are the last visible signs of deeply rooted emotional crises. Likewise, Brandon Bays, author of *The Journey*, talks about holding on to deep wounds and how old grievances find root in our bodies and cause disease.

Look after your health

Undoubtedly your health is your biggest asset. When I meet people who blatantly do not take care of themselves and continue to expect their body to function fully, I am saddened by their level of disconnection.

The way you take care of yourself is a reflection of how much you care. When you binge eat, drink, smoke, stay up late and diminish your sleep time you are on the slippery slope. Just like the negative voices in your head that we spoke about in Chapter 4, this is another form of self-sabotage. When you burn the candle at both ends, you begin to deplete your energy reserves. This, in turn, leads you to feeling irritable, tired and not being able to operate at your optimum level. This is when you leave yourself wide open to colds and illnesses. If you want a life that works, where you feel motivated and energized, you need a body that works: the two go hand in hand.

There are umpteen books and articles written about what we should be eating and drinking. There is always going to be the latest fad diet, one minute telling us to up our protein and the next telling us to cut out carbs. Scary headlines abound, like red meat is linked to cancer so we should cut it out, only to find out a few months later that it's good for us in moderation. Life can be very confusing at times. It is important to tune into our unique needs and learn to follow our common sense and good council. But beyond a wholesome discipline, be mindful that a good healthy diet, which avoids processed foods and centres around good fresh food in season with plenty of water, is obviously going to pay dividends.

Anything you overeat could harm you, even oranges. If you ate enough of them they could make you obese, do you remember the story of the fat man who died of overeating oranges? Moderation and portion control are great disciplines; you can have anything you want as long as you don't overdo it.

However, there is no need for me to go into any depth on what you can do in the area of diet as there are so many experts who have written volumes on nutritional balance and detox programmes. At the risk of sounding controversial, *diets don't work on their own*!

Take regular exercise
Walk the dog, have a swim or go to the gym. Find some regular activity you enjoy and make sure you do it for 20 minutes, at least, three times per week. When we are moving, we become more creative. Walking in nature is good for our soul and clears the head of noise. As you breathe in the fresh air, you are giving yourself an opportunity to clear your head.

Oxygen, being outdoors and moving all help with staying flexible physically and mentally. If you sit on a sofa all day watching daytime reality TV, this is a recipe for disaster. These programmes are designed to keep us glued to the box. Make a rule to watch less and move more. Twenty minutes out in the garden and fresh air will do you a lot more good than sitting inside plonked on a sofa. I notice that my kids, left to their own devices, can sit watching screens for far too long. When we are in front of a screen, we become unavailable and withdrawn. When my son spends more than an hour on his laptop he becomes addicted to the buzz that it gives him, and that is bad for him in the long run. Just as children need to let off steam and run and play in the outdoors, we need our equivalent. Avoid the pull to become a couch potato as this is more likely to make you feel low and out of sorts.

If you have not been physically active for some time, gentle, steady progress is the key. Be careful not to overdo it at first, and check it out with your doctor before you start or if you are unsure. A good way to start exercising is to carry on with your everyday routine, but do things in a way that requires a bit more energy. Then build these activities into your daily lifestyle.

Walking is often a good way to start. Why not:

- Try getting off the bus or train a stop early and walk the rest of the way.
- Leave your car at home one day a week and walk all, or part, of the way, to work.

Get more sleep

It is often quoted that Margaret Thatcher could get by on just four hours of sleep a night. Many a famous person who brags about this may well be telling the truth. What we don't know is how many cat naps they have during the day. Or very possibly they were never aware of their levels of sleepiness because it had become the norm for them. Everyone's sleep quota is different. I imagine you have friends who pop off to bed at 11 pm every night and are as bright as buttons at 6 am while you feel that you need a few more hours. Find out what works for you and, more importantly, what leaves you feeling refreshed when you wake up.

Too little sleep will rob you of a vital healing ingredient. Research shows that depleted sleep weakens the immune system, which leads to – you've guessed it – illness and disease.

Don't be fooled into thinking that you can take sleep medications or catch up on your sleep at weekends. This is not the case. What needs to happen, as I have said, is for you to look at the whole of you and to make changes that promote good sleep practices.

Sleep is one of the most important gifts that you can give yourself. Where you sleep and the environment you create is a signal to your body that it's time to drift off. What immediate changes can you make to your bedroom today?

Next I want to ask you what you could achieve if you slept better. Make that the prime motivation for getting a good night's sleep.

Book in regular check-ups
Every 10,000 or so miles, I am sure you get your car checked; and every week you look at water and oil levels. How often do you do that for yourself? There is a saying that illness is the Western man's meditation. In the West, we typically only go to the doctor when we are ill. That is too late. Ignore the signs at your peril. Find a way to enjoy having regular tune-ups.

Spiritual

Don't forget your values
We started this book with your values. This is because they are the foundation for your life. Living by them enriches everything.

Check your vision board
Did you do a vision board? If yes, get it out and check that it is in alignment with your values. Your vision and values enable

you to keep your goals and aspirations alive. Remember, this powerful yet simple asset will support you and your greatest aspirations, experiences and the life you want to create. Put it somewhere that you get to see it every day and make sure to update it on an ongoing basis. This will help keep the dream alive and maintain your energy and focus. Feel free to share it with your friends and family. If anyone sniggers at any of your life goals, be very wary of them!

Show gratitude

When you live your life by your values and can visualize what you want, it will come to you. What is important is that you acknowledge and show gratitude. Remember that what you focus on is what you get. However, deciding to be grateful for what you have will bring happiness to your life, and when you are happy you can share that with others. You may not be able to bring about world peace, but you can be a catalyst for others.

 Over to you

What are you grateful for?

What are you grateful for right now in your life? Try this week-long experiment. Every day, write down five things that you are grateful for and then record how you feel at the end of it.

Practise mindful activities

There is something deeply satisfying about slowing it down. I for one no longer want to feel the burn; rather I want to simmer slowly and enjoy life. These are some of the ways that I practise being mindful.

Try yoga

This is a great way of connecting with your inner peace and flexibility. Yoga is a way of life; it is not just about poses (asanas). It is wonderful for stretching, balancing and deep breathing, which when combined connect you to your spiritual energy. At first, you will be very aware of the chatter in your head but, with practise, you can learn to quieten the noise and connect to your breathing and your body. Yoga is a great workout for the physical body but, more importantly, the mind. Create a space in your house that always has a yoga mat available, a block and perhaps some candles so that you can turn some simple yoga asana into a spiritual practice. Awaken your senses by burning scented oils and candles. We can elevate the simplest routines into a spiritual practice if we approach it with reverence and care.

Meditate

Contrary to the popular belief of those who do not meditate, you do not have to sit crossed-legged for hours and go 'om ... '.

There are numerous books, tapes and people who could help you start to experiment with meditation.[1] If you take to it, you may wish to create a regular practice or ritual. Make a space in your home that becomes your own little sanctuary.

Keep a journal

Writing regularly in a journal helps you capture new ideas and also assists you in recording your journey. Make sure you write down things you are grateful for; if you count your blessings regularly and note the miracles that are happening

[1] Visit my website to download the meditation from the resources section.

in your life on a regular basis you will begin to feel happier, more fulfilled and satisfied. You will also be able to see how far you have come in reaching and attaining your goals.

Appreciate and validate people

Make more time to appreciate the great people in your life. Yes, they may do irritating things from time to time, as you do; however, if you can separate the behaviour from the person and see their actions as their response to their experiences, it should help you to be more understanding. A spoonful of sugar sprinkled on some of your relationships will go a long way. Let people know that they are making a difference to you.

Spend time with family and friends

These are the people that nurture you, and now that you have removed the unhealthy relationships you can spend more of your precious energy and time with them instead. These are the people that fill you with love. Treasure them.

Come from abundance – there is plenty to go around

You get in life what you expect. People who have a healthy relationship with money and resources tend to experience it coming towards them easily. Others do the opposite and are always moaning about what they don't have. I have noticed that these people also tend to be tight with money and quite penny pinching. Generosity and spiritual wealth have nothing to do with the amount of money you have. I have known people who are of relatively modest means yet they are always offering to buy the next round of drinks or to pay the bill, buy generous presents and never forget to send a card or a present.

Others who have plenty of money may never offer to pay; where they live in their heads is a poverty stricken world.

Remember the story of Silas Marner? He died hoarding his gold.

Money is a facility that, like water, flows to you when it is needed – assuming you have a healthy mindset about it. Like water, if you hoard it, and it never moves, it becomes stagnant. I have always felt that my trigger for money coming towards me is when I have a purpose for it. Generating great reasons to have money and positive visualizations is the best way to create it.

There is enough to go round; always celebrate other people's good fortune. Resentfulness, jealousy and bitterness will only reconfirm your deep-rooted unworthiness to receive. By being jealous and resentful, we are saying we will never have. Guess what? We will be right about that. Remember that we create our own reality and everything we think about and how we expect our lives to unfold will probably manifest.

Better to be joyous and celebrate other people's good fortune, and use this as inspiration to go for it yourself with a positive mindset of 'I can and I will'.

 Over to you

Abundance visualization

Your wealth consciousness is not dependent on money; your wealth is dependent on how abundant and wealthy you are in your mind.

Imagine that you are looking out onto a vast ocean, knowing that this abundance is available to each and every one of us.

Now imagine wanting to capture some of that ocean; consider what you can use to gather the abundance of the ocean.

Will you get a cup, a bucket, a barrel; or will you have a pipe that links it in some way to you in your home, so you have a never-ending supply as you need it?

Now look around at the people about you: they all want some of the ocean too.

Will their getting some deprive you? Is it worth you being jealous of how much they have in their buckets? Will being jealous or pushing them away give you more? NO.

There is plenty to go around. Take what you need and come back when you want more in the certainty that the ocean will always be there for you when you choose to tap into its abundant flow.

IF YOU WERE ON YOUR DEATH BED

Taking care of yourself physically, mentally and spiritually will keep you on your path of personal motivation, meaning and purpose. I hope that reading this book has helped you grasp the importance of connecting to your core values. Making sure you live your life with these values as centre stage can only result in a meaningful and motivated life.

An important question to ask yourself at this stage is: If you were on your deathbed today, would you be celebrating the wonderful life you have had, the rich relationships you have developed with family and friends, the contribution you have made to the people around you? Or will you be looking back in regret? Regret, perhaps, that you spent too much time waiting for the right time to arrive when you could finally focus on being happy – well, this is it.

MOTIVATE YOURSELF NOW

Take this opportunity to motivate yourself and begin now to ensure you are creating a life of meaning with no regrets. If *Motivate Yourself* has helped you to highlight what's important to you in life, then spending more time and energy in the pursuit of those goals can only result in more motivation and fulfilment. If you arrived at this book with your motivation and happiness just out of reach, then I am confident you now have the tools and principles to activate the new behaviour that will achieve the results you are yearning for.

My purpose throughout this book has been to give you a distillation of my life's work. To share the tools and principles that have helped me create a meaningful life with motivation and purpose.

Don't waste any more time wondering if you are good enough, worthy enough or have the skills to achieve what you want – just go for it. Life is too short to waste time doubting yourself.

If I had listened to my RAT and saboteur voices, I would never have even started this book, let alone completed it. So if the words printed on these pages have helped you change one limiting belief, or encouraged you to shine the light on one core value you want to express more fully in your life, then this book has achieved its purpose.

Remember: everything starts with one small step, and that's all it takes.

Believe in yourself, good luck!

Donovan's Ten Motivational Principles

....

1. Spend some time every day being silent.
2. Be up to date in all your relationships; toxic friends and family contaminate your energy.
3. Aim high and do your best with all your endeavours; remember you get in life what you expect and go for.
4. Express yourself fully in spite of perceived judgement.
5. Try something new and leave your comfort zone regularly, this is where growth and magic happens.
6. Express more love, appreciation and gratitude.
7. If today was your last day, how would you be spending it?
8. Be kind to yourself and be at peace with your soul.
9. Everyone has a voice – listen, and be heard.
10. Be positive, choose to be happy.

References

Introduction

Ware, Bronnie, *The Top 5 Regrets of the Dying* (Hay House, 2012). For more information about Bronnie Ware and *The Top 5 Regrets of the Dying*, visit hayhouse.com.au or bronnieware.com.

Chapter 3

Goleman, Daniel. *Emotional Intelligence* (Bloomsbury Publishing PLC, 1996).

Chapter 4

Hay, Julie. *Drivers – and Working Styles: An Essay*. 2013. http://www.juliehay.org/uploads/1/2/2/9/12294841/drivers__working_stlyes_-_an_essay.pdf.

Chapter 5

Robinson, Ken. 'Do schools kill creativity?', TED talk, February 2006. https://www.ted.com/talks/ken_robinson_says_schools_kill_creativity?language=en.

Chapter 8

Bays, Brandon. *The Journey* (Harper Collins, 1999).
Hay, Louise. *You Can Heal Your Life* (Hay House, 1984).

Resources and Next Steps

HEAD OVER TO WWW.ANDRODONOVAN.COM WHERE YOU WILL FIND:

- Community information, support, tools, videos, courses and other materials that will support your personal development.
- A sign-up box for worksheets and webinars.
- How to become a certified 'motivate-yourself' coach/facilitator.
- Details on joining the Donovan Academy for Coaches online programme.
- And much more!

For details on how to hire Andro Donovan for retreats, coaching you and your teams, as well as for corporate transformation programmes and management team building, please visit www.androdonovan.com or contact Andro at Andro@androdonovan.co.uk. Tweet her at @AndroDonovan8.

CREATE A MY PEER GROUP IN YOUR AREA

To create a MY peer group I suggest:

1. Start a book group using *Motivate Yourself* and put it into practice together. This will provide a regular group for you to tap into and help you stay on your path.
2. Spread the word and invite other like-minded people to join your group or start another group.
3. Get in touch with Andro if you need further support or you want to have a retreat.

About the Author

Andro is a globally sought after facilitator, speaker, author and consultant. She specializes in coaching high-performing CEOs and entrepreneurs to become more effective leaders with a stronger sense of meaning and purpose in their lives. She combines her 20 years' experience as a management consultant with her natural insight and affinity with all types of people to help her clients gain greater influence, effectiveness and perspective.

Andro is known for creating safe environments where deep personal transformation can happen individually and in collaboration. She has worked extensively with cross-cultural groups on a global level, empowering top peer group connection and teamwork.

She is best known for her life-changing fulfilment retreats for top executive forums around the world, who explore their own personal development, self-actualization and making a difference.

From her background of teaching English Literature to disengaged school students, and inspiring them about their life and future, Andro went on to work in a management consulting practice for a number of years.

In 1990, she set up the Hemingways Consulting Group, a leadership development and corporate transformation consultancy.

After 15 years of working with blue chip companies in the city as a management consultant, and witnessing many burnt-out CEOs, Andro set up her executive coaching practice.

Andro lives in Wiltshire with her husband Tim and her two children Bella and Dimitri and their dog Coco. When she is not working she loves to go on family excursions along the southern coast, and enjoys exploring historical buildings, as architecture and restoration are two of her main interests.

Andro can be contacted at:
www.androdonovan.com
www.Motivate-Yourself.co.uk
Andro@androdonovan.co.uk
@AndroDonovan8

Andro Donovan BA Hons, BEd, Co-active CTI.
Certified YPO facilitator [Young Presidents
Organisation] and EO [Entrepreneurs Organisation]
Accredited Vistage speaker

Acknowledgements

This book is the culmination of a journey shared with many people who have inspired me, and whose work and teachings have influenced and added value to my own personal growth and development. I am most grateful to all my friends and colleagues, who have engaged and discussed many of the ideas explored in this book with me over the years.

Special thanks go to Jacqui Malpass, my coach, who was always there to encourage me, guide me and read through copious amounts of copy. Without you I would have given up after the first chapter.

Andy Maslen, for giving me his perspective on how to approach the publishing world.

Daniel Priestly, who first inspired me to write my book with his *Key Person of Influence* book.

Annie Knight, Commissioning Editor, who believed in my book concept at proposal stage, and latterly to Jenny Ng for her gentle and respectful editing of my manuscript.

I am also deeply indebted to my loyal clients who have engaged with my methods, participated fully during the workshops and have written back to me letting me know that I and this material makes a difference to them.

Acknowledgements

My love goes to my precious children Bella, and Dimitri, who were so patient, even when Mummy was not always available for family outings due to her writing schedule.

Finally, and most importantly, my gratitude goes to my beloved husband, friend and soul mate, Tim. Thank you for reading my manuscript, for believing in me, and above all for being my rock when I lost my way.

Index